EASY
HEBREW
PHRASE BOOK
Over 770 Basic Phrases
For Everyday Use

DOVER PUBLICATIONS, INC.
NEW YORK

Copyright

Copyright © 1962, 1986, 1995 by Dover Publications, Inc.
All rights reserved under Pan American and International Copyright Conventions.

Published in Canada by General Publishing Company, Ltd., 30 Lesmill Road, Don Mills, Toronto, Ontario.
Published in the United Kingdom by Constable and Company, Ltd., 3 The Lanchesters, 162–164 Fulham Palace Road, London W6 9ER.

Bibliographical Note

The material in this book was originally published by Dover in 1962 as part of a manual to accompany a recording entitled *Listen & Learn Modern Hebrew*. The English outline was prepared by the editorial staff of Dover Publications, Inc. The Hebrew translation and transliteration were prepared by Menahem Mansoor.

Library of Congress Cataloging-in-Publication Data

Mansoor, Menahem.
 Easy Hebrew phrase book : over 770 basic phrases for everyday use.
  p. cm.
 Material in this book was originally published by Menahem Mansoor and the editorial staff of Dover publications as record accompanying manual entitled Listen & learn modern Hebrew.
 Includes index.
 ISBN 0-486-28556-1 (pkb.)
 1. Hebrew language—Conversation and phrase books—English. I. Mansoor, Menahem. Listen & learn modern Hebrew. II. Title.
PJ4573.M36 1995
492.4'83421—dc20
                 94-43467
                 CIP

Manufactured in the United States of America
Dover Publications, Inc., 31 East 2nd Street, Mineola, N.Y. 11501

CONTENTS

INTRODUCTION

This book is designed to teach you the basic words, phrases and sentences that you will need for simple everyday communication in Israel. It does not attempt to teach you the grammatical structure of Hebrew, but instead helps you to express your needs and handle problems encountered while traveling.

The value of the book rests as much on what is omitted as on what is included. An effort has been made to include only those phrases pertinent to the needs of the traveler. You will find the phrase "May I have some small change" (a frequent need in travel), but do not expect to find a sentence like "This is the pen of my aunt." Furthermore, since the material presented here is not cumulative, as it is in conventional foreign-language courses, you need not start at the beginning. Study whichever phrases will be the most useful to you.

The focus of instruction is on what *you* will say. However, the section entitled "Making Yourself Understood," which contains such vital phrases as "Please speak more slowly" and "Repeat it, please," will aid you in understanding others.

This book is complete in itself and is meant to be used for reference and study. Read it at odd moments and try to learn ten or fifteen phrases a day. Also, be sure to take the manual with you when you go abroad. All that you have learned will be available for reference and review.

The book is designed to help you form additional Hebrew sentences from the sentences it provides. You can do this by substituting a new word for a given word in a familiar sentence. In sentences where this is possible, the candidate for substitution appears in brackets, and is sometimes followed by possible alternatives. For example,

> I am [a student]
> —a teacher
> —a businessman

provides three sentences: "I am a student," "I am a teacher" and "I am a businessman."

Another especially helpful feature of the manual is the extensive topic and word index beginning on page 57. Notice that each entry in the book is numbered and that the index refers to these numbers. This enables you to locate information you need quickly, without having to search the entire page.

To avoid ambiguity, embarrassment and incorrect usage, we have used the following scheme to indicate clearly the correct gender wherever necessary:

(M.)	male speaking to anyone
(F.)	female speaking to anyone
(TO M.)	anyone speaking to a male
(TO F.)	anyone speaking to female.

Where an alternate gender is given for a word only the initial form is recorded. Where no gender is indicated the statement may be considered general; that is, it may be spoken by male or female to male or female.

HEBREW PRONUNCIATION

The pronunciation used throughout the *Easy Hebrew Phrase Book* is Sefardic, that of contemporary Israel. The manual uses a phonetic transcription as an aid to correct pronunciation. (See "Scheme of Pronunciation," below.) Stressed syllables (which in Hebrew occur most often at the ends of words) are written in capital letters in the transcription.

Most Hebrew sounds will present no difficulty for English speakers. However, many Hebrew sounds have subtle differences in pronunciation from their English counterparts. Those sounds that do not occur in English are marked with an arrow in the Scheme of Pronunciation.

SCHEME OF PRONUNCIATION

Hebrew Letter	Transcrip- tion	Example	Notes
א	—	silent	
בּ	*b*	as in *b*oy	
ב	*v*	as in *v*ast	
ג	*g*	as in *g*irl, never as in *g*iant	
ד	*d*	as in *d*ance	
ה	*h*	as in *h*ot	Silent only when final letter of word.

Hebrew Letter	Transcription	Example	Notes
ו	v	as in vast	Also used in vowels וֹ and וּ.
ז	z	as in zoo	
➡ ח	kh		No English equivalent. Like ch in Scottish loch or German Bach.
ט	t	as in sting	
י	y	as in young	Also used in vowels יִ.., יֵ., and יְ_.
כ	k	as in skin	Never silent as in knee.
➡*ך כ	kh		(See note on ח, above.)
ל	l	as in lip	Pronounced farther forward in the mouth than English l.
מ ם*	m	as in meat	
*ן נ	n	as in note	
ס	s	as in sea	
ע	—	silent	Some native speakers may pronounce this like the gulping sound (glottal stop) that replaces the tt in bottle in some New Yorkers' speech.
פ	p	as in spin	
*ף פ	f	as in first	
*ץ צ	ts	as in hits	Pronounced as a unit.
ק	k	as in skin	
➡ ר	r		Produced by vibrating the uvula against the back of the tongue, as in French. A gargling r sound.
שׁ	sh	as in she	
שׂ	s	as in sea	
ת or תּ	t	as in sting	

*This is the form of the letter when it appears at the end of a word.

NOTE: Every Hebrew letter is a consonant.

Vowel Sounds

The vowels of Hebrew are indicated by means of diacritical marks written under the consonants they are to follow. In order to write a vowel, therefore, it is helpful to combine it with a consonant from the alphabet given above. We have used א in the examples given below, because it has no sound of its own.

Hebrew Vowel	Transcription	Example	Notes
אָ ,אַ ,אָ	ă	like *a* in *a*bet	This vowel sound varies in the length of its duration. This distinction, which never affects the meaning of words, is becoming rather vague and haphazard in modern spoken Hebrew.
אֵ ,אֶ	ĕ	as in g*e*t	
→ אֶ	ĕ	like *e* in g*e*t or like *a* in f*a*te	Varies from speaker to speaker. The pronunciation like *e* in g*e*t is considered by many to be the more "modern" and "native" sound. When pronouncing this vowel with the sound of *a* in f*a*te, take care to make it a pure vowel; avoid ending with a sound of *ee*, as is usual in English: that is, keep the sound short and clipped (not *fay-eet*).
אֵי	ay	as in pl*ay*	
אִי ,אֵי	ee	as in sw*ee*t	
אַי	ī	as in *i*ce	
→ אוֹ ,אֹ	ŏ	like *ou* in *ou*ght or like *o* in h*o*me	Varies. The pronunciation like *ou* in *ou*ght is considered more "modern" and "native." This sound should not be drawled; it often approaches the *u* in f*u*n. When pronouncing this vowel with the sound of *o* in h*o*me, make it a clipped, pure vowel; avoid ending with a sound of *oo* (not *ho-oom*).
אֳ	ŏ	like *ou* in *ou*ght	Of very short duration.

Hebrew Letter	Transcription	Example	Notes
אֹ ,אוּ	oo	as in boot	Not as in look.
אוּי	ooey	as in gooey	
→ אֱ	sometimes ⌣, sometimes not transcribed	like second e in secretary or preferable	A very short indistinct sound like the colorless English vowel in the examples given. When it occurs at the end of a word or syllable it is generally not pronounced at all, and in these cases it does not appear in our transcription; thus, אָתְּ ăt, אִשְׁתִּי eesh-TEE. When it occurs between consonants at the beginning of a syllable, we have transcribed it by a ligature; thus, לְהַכִּיר l⌣hă-KEER, בְּנֵי b⌣nee.

NOTE: When vowel sounds come together in a Hebrew word, each one retains its individuality much more than in the case of English diphthongs, and the glide between the vowels is much less pronounced than it is in English.

SOCIAL CONVERSATION

1. Hello.
שָׁלוֹם.
shă-LŌM.

2. Good morning.
בֹּקֶר טוֹב.
BŌ-kĕr tŏv.

3. Good evening.
עֶרֶב טוֹב.
Ĕ-rĕv tŏv.

4. Good night.
לֵיל מְנוּחָה.
layl mǝnoo-KHĂ.

5. Goodbye.
שָׁלוֹם.
shă-LŌM.

6. I'll see you later.
לְהִתְרָאוֹת.
Lǝheet-ră-ŌT.

7. I wish to make an appointment with Mr. Allon.
אֲנִי (רוֹצֶה) (רוֹצָה) לִקְבֹּעַ רַאֲיוֹן עִם מַר אַלוֹן.
ă-NEE (rŏ-TSĔ m.) (rŏ-TSĂ f.) leek-BŌ-ă rĕ-ă-YŎN eem măr ă-LŎN.

8. May I introduce [Mrs. Doron]?
נָא לְהַכִּיר אֶת [הַגְּבֶרֶת דּוֹרוֹן].
nă Lǝhă-KEER ĕt [hă-Gǝ-VĔ-rĕt dö-RŎN].

9. —— my wife.
אִשְׁתִּי.
eesh-TEE.

10. —— my husband.
בַּעֲלִי.
bă-ă-LEE.

11. —— my mother.
אִמִּי.
ee-MEE.

12. —— my father.
אָבִי.
ă-VEE.

13. —— my daughter.
בִּתִּי.
bee-TEE.

14. —— my son.
בְּנִי.
bǝnee.

15. —— my child.
יַלְדִּי.
yăl-DEE.

16. —— my sister.
אֲחוֹתִי.
ă-khö-TEE.

17. —— my brother.
אָחִי.
ă-KHEE.

18. May I introduce my friend?
נָא לְהַכִּיר אֶת (חֲבֵרִי) (חֲבֶרְתִּי).
nă Lǝhă-KEER ĕt (khă-vĕ-REE m.) (khă-vĕr-TEE f.).

19. I am glad to meet you.
נָעִים מְאֹד.
nă-EEM mǝŏd.

20. How are you?
מַה (שְׁלוֹמְךָ) (שְׁלוֹמֵךְ)
mă (shǝlö-Mǝ KHĂ to m.) (shǝlö-MĔKH to f.)?

21. Very well, thanks, and you?
טוֹב, תּוֹדָה.   וּמַה (שְׁלוֹמְךָ) (שְׁלוֹמֵךְ)
tŏv, tö-DĂ.   oo-MĂ (shǝlö-Mǝ KHĂ to m.) (shǝlö-MĔKH to f)?

22. All right.

הַכֹּל בְּסֵדֶר.

hă-KŌL B̄ SĔ-dĕr.

23. How is your family?

מַה שְׁלוֹם הַמִּשְׁפָּחָה?

mă sh lŏm hă-meesh-pă-KHĂ?

24. Please sit down.

נָא לָשֶׁבֶת.

nă lă-SHĔ-vĕt.

25. I enjoyed myself very much.

נֶהֱנֵיתִי מְאֹד.

nĕ-hĕ-NAY-tee m ŏd.

26. Regards to your uncle.

דְּרִישַׁת שָׁלוֹם (לְדוֹדְךָ) לְדוֹדֵךְ.

d ree-SHĂT shă-LŌM (l dŏ-D KHĂ TO M.*) (l dŏ-DĔKH* TO F.*).*

27. Regards to your aunt.

דְּרִישַׁת שָׁלוֹם (לְדוֹדָתְךָ) (לְדוֹדָתֵךְ).

d ree-SHĂT shă-LŌM (l dŏ-dăt-KHĂ TO M.*) (l dŏ-dă-TĔKH* TO F.*).*

28. Come visit us again.

(בֹּאִי) (בֹּא) לְבַקֵּר אוֹתָנוּ שׁוּב.

(BŌ-ee TO F.*)(bŏ* TO M.*) l vă-KĔR ŏ-TĂ-noo shoov.*

29. May I visit you (PL.) again?

הַאִם אוּכַל לְבַקֵּר אֶצְלְכֶם שׁוּב?

hă-EEM oo-KHĂL l vă-KĔR ĕts-L KHĔM shoov?

30. I like you very much.

(אַתְּ מוֹצֵאת)(אַתָּה מוֹצֵא) חֵן בְּעֵינַי מְאֹד.

(ăt mŏ-TSĔT TO F.*) (ă-TĂ mŏ-TSĔ* TO M.*) khĕn b ay-NI m ŏd.*

31. Congratulations!

מַזָּל טוֹב!

mă-Z̧ĂL tŏv!

32. All the best!

כָּל טוּב!

kŏl toov!

33. Happy New Year.

שָׁנָה טוֹבָה.

shă-NĂ tŏ-VĂ.

34. Happy festival.

חַג שָׂמֵחַ.

khăg să-MĔ-ăkh.

35. A Sabbath of peace.

שַׁבָּת שָׁלוֹם.

shă-BĂT shă-LŌM.

36. Happy week.

שָׁבוּעַ טוֹב.

shă-VOO-ă tŏv.

PERSONAL MATTERS

37. What is your name?

מַה (שִׁמְךָ) (שְׁמֵךְ)

mă (shee-M KHĂ TO M.*) (sh mĕkh* TO F.*)?*

38. My name is [Daniel].

שְׁמִי [דָּנִיאֵל].

sh mee [dă-nee-YĔL].

39. I am 20 years old.

אֲנִי (בֶּן) (בַּת) עֶשְׂרִים.

ă-NEE (bĕn M.*) (băt* F.*) ĕs-REEM.*

40. I am an American citizen.

אֲנִי (אֶזְרָח אֲמֶרִיקָנִי) (אֶזְרָחִית אֲמֶרִיקָנִית).

ă-NEE (ĕz-RĂKH ă-mĕ-ree-kă-NEE M.) (ĕz-ră-KHEET ă-mĕ-ree-kă-NEET F.).

41. My mailing address is [20 Herzl Street].

הַכְּתֹבֶת שֶׁלִּי הִיא רְחוֹב הֶרְצֵל עֶשְׂרִים.

hă-K⌣TŎ-vĕt shĕ-LEE hee [r⌣khŏv hĕrtsl ĕs-REEM].

42. I am a college student.

אֲנִי (סְטוּדֶנְט) (סְטוּדֶנְטִית).

ă-NEE (stoo-DĔNT M.) (stoo-DĔN-teet F.).

43. I am a high-school student.

אֲנִי (תַּלְמִיד) (תַּלְמִידָה) בְּבֵית-סֵפֶר תִּיכוֹן.

ă-NEE (tăl-MEED M.) (tăl-mee-DĂ F.) b⌣vayt-SĔ-fĕr tee-KHŎN.

44. I am a teacher.

אֲנִי (מוֹרֶה) (מוֹרָה).

ă-NEE (mŏ-RĔ M.) (mŏ-RĂ F.).

45. I am a businessman.

אֲנִי אִישׁ עֲסָקִים.

ă-NEE eesh ă-să-KEEM.

46. I am a friend of Robert Cohen.

אֲנִי (חָבֵר) (חֲבֵרָה) שֶׁל רוֹבֶּרְט כֹּהֵן.

ă-NEE (khă-VĔR M.) (khă-vĕ-RĂ F.) shĕl RŎ-bĕrt KŎ-hĕn.

47. He works [for the Rimon Company].

הוּא עוֹבֵד [בְּחֶבְרַת רִמּוֹן].

hoo ŏ-VĔD [b⌣khĕv-RĂT ree-MŎN].

48. I am here [on vacation].

אֲנִי כָּאן [בְּחֻפְשָׁה].

ă-NEE kăn [b⌣khoof-SHĂ].

49. ———— on business.

בְּעִנְיְנֵי עֲסָקִים.

b⌣een-yă-NAY ă-să-KEEM.

50. I am traveling to Jerusalem.

אֲנִי (נוֹסֵעַ) (נוֹסַעַת) לִירוּשָׁלַיִם.

ă-NEE (nŏ-SĔ-ă M.) (nŏ-SĂ-ăt F.) lee-roo-shă-LĂ-yeem.

51. I am in a hurry.

אֲנִי (מְמַהֵר) (מְמַהֶרֶת).

ă-NEE (m⌣mă-HĔR M.) (m⌣mă-HĔ-rĕt F.).

52. I am hungry.

אֲנִי (רָעֵב) (רְעֵבָה).

ă-NEE (ră-ĔV M.) (r⌣ĕ-VĂ F.).

53. I am thirsty.

אֲנִי (צָמֵא) (צְמֵאָה).

ă-NEE (tsă-MĔ M.) (ts⌣mĕ-Ă F.).

4

54. I am busy.

אֲנִי (עָסוּק) (עֲסוּקָה).

ă-NEE (ă-SOOK M.) (ă-soo-KĂ F.).

55. I am tired.

אֲנִי (עָיֵף) (עֲיֵפָה).

ă-NEE (ă-YĚF M.) (ă-yĕ-FĂ F.).

56. I am sorry.

אֲנִי (מִצְטַעֵר) (מִצְטַעֶרֶת).

ă-NEE (meets-tă-ĚR M.) (meets-tă-Ě-rĕt F.).

57. We were not pleased.

לֹא הָיִינוּ (מְרֻצִּים) (מְרֻצּוֹת).

lō hă-YEE-noo (m⁀roo-TSEEM M.) (m⁀roo-TSŌT F.).

MAKING YOURSELF UNDERSTOOD

58. Do you speak English?

הַאִם (אַתָּה מְדַבֵּר) (אַתְּ מְדַבֶּרֶת) אַנְגְּלִית?

hă-EEM (ă-TĂ m⁀dă-BĚR TO M.) (ăt m⁀dă-BĚ-rĕt TO F.) ăng-LEET?

59. Does anyone here speak [English]?

הַאִם מְדַבֵּר כָּאן מִישֶׁהוּ [אַנְגְּלִית]?

hă-EEM m⁀dă-BĚR kăn MEE-shĕ-hoo [ăng-LEET]?

60. I read only English.

אֲנִי (קוֹרֵא) (קוֹרֵאת) רַק אַנְגְּלִית.

ă-NEE (kŏ-RĚ M.) (kŏ-RĚT F.) răk ăng-LEET.

61. I speak a little Hebrew.

אֲנִי (מְדַבֵּר) (מְדַבֶּרֶת) קְצָת עִבְרִית.

ă-NEE (m⁀dă-BĚR M.) (m⁀dă-BĚ-rĕt F.) k⁀tsăt eev-REET.

62. Speak more slowly, please.

(דַּבֵּר) (דַּבְּרִי) יוֹתֵר לְאַט, בְּבַקָשָׁה.

(dă-BĚR TO M.) (dă-B⁀REE TO F.) yŏ-TĚR l⁀ăt, b⁀vă-kă-SHĂ.

63. I understand.

אֲנִי (מֵבִין) (מְבִינָה).

ă-NEE (mĕ-VEEN M.) (m⁀vee-NĂ F.).

64. I do not understand.

אֵינֶנִּי (מֵבִין) (מְבִינָה).

ay-NĚ-nee (mĕ-VEEN M.) (m⁀vee-NĂ F.).

65. Do you understand me?

הַאִם (אַתָּה מֵבִין) (אַתְּ מְבִינָה) אוֹתִי?

hă-EEM (ă-TĂ mĕ-VEEN TO M.) (ăt m⁀vee-NĂ TO F.) ŏ-TEE?

66. I know.
אֲנִי (יוֹדֵעַ) (יוֹדַעַת).
ă-NEE (yŏ-DĔ-ă M.) (yŏ-DĂ-ăt F.).

67. I do not know.
אֵינֶנִּי (יוֹדֵעַ) (יוֹדַעַת).
ay-NĔ-nee (yŏ-DĔ-ă M.) (yŏ-DĂ-ăt F.).

68. I think so.
אֲנִי (חוֹשֵׁב) (חוֹשֶׁבֶת) כָּךְ.
ă-NEE (khŏ-SHĔV M.) (khŏ-SHĔ-vĕt F.) kăkh.

69. I do not think so.
אֵינֶנִּי (חוֹשֵׁב) (חוֹשֶׁבֶת) כָּךְ.
ay-NĔ-nee (khŏ-SHĔV M.) (khŏ-SHĔ-vĕt F.) kăkh.

70. Repeat it, please.
(חֲזֹר) (חִזְרִי) עַל זֶה, בְּבַקָּשָׁה.
(khă-ZŎR TO M.) (khee-Z~REE TO F.) ăl zĕ, b~vă-kă-SHĂ.

71. Write it down, please.
(רְשֹׁם) (רִשְׁמִי) אֶת זֶה, בְּבַקָּשָׁה.
(r~shŏm TO M.) (ree-SH~MEE TO F.) ĕt zĕ, b~vă-kă-SHĂ.

72. What is the meaning of [this word]?
מַה פֵּרוּשׁ [הַמִּלָּה הַזֹּאת]?
mă pĕ-ROOSH [hă-mee-LĂ hă-ZŎT]?

73. What is that?
מַה זֶה?
mă zĕ?

74. What is this?
מַה זֶה?
mă zĕ?

75. How do you say ["pencil"] in Hebrew?
אֵיךְ אוֹמְרִים [«פֶּנְסִיל»] בְּעִבְרִית?
aykh ŏ-M~REEM ["pencil"] b~eev-REET?

76. How do you write this word?
אֵיךְ כּוֹתְבִים אֶת הַמִּלָּה הַזֹּאת?
aykh kŏ-T~VEEM ĕt hă-mee-LĂ hă-ZŎT?

GENERAL EXPRESSIONS

77. Yes.
כֵּן.
kĕn.

78. No.
לֹא.
lŏ.

79. Perhaps.
אוּלַי.
oo-LI.

80. Please.
בְּבַקָּשָׁה.
b~vă-kă-SHĂ.

81. Excuse me.
סְלִיחָה.
s~lee-KHĂ.

82. Thanks very much.
תּוֹדָה רַבָּה.
tŏ-DĂ ră-BĂ.

83. You are welcome.
עַל לֹא דָבָר.
ăl lŏ dă-VĂR.

84. All right.
בְּסֵדֶר.
B~SĔ-dĕr.

85. Very good.
טוֹב מְאֹד.
tŏv m~ŏd.

86. It doesn't matter.

אֵין דָּבָר.

ayn dă-VĂR.

87. Please do not bother.

אָנָּא אַל (תַּטְרִיחַ אֶת עַצְמְךָ) (תַּטְרִיחִי אֶת עַצְמֵךְ).

Ă-nă ăl (tăt-REE-ăkh ĕt ăts-M‿KHĂ TO M.) (tăt-REE-khee ĕt ăts-MĔKH TO F.).

88. Please do not worry.

אָנָּא אַל (תִּדְאַג) (תִּדְאֲגִי).

Ă-nă ăl (teed-ĂG TO M.) (teed-ă-GEE TO F.).

89. Who are you?

מִי (אַתָּה) (אַתְּ)?

mee (ă-TĂ TO M.) (ăt TO F.)?

90. Who is this boy?

מִי הַיֶּלֶד הַזֶּה?

mee hă-YĔ-lĕd hă-ZĔ?

91. Who is this girl?

מִי הַיַּלְדָּה הַזֹּאת?

mee hă-yăl-DĂ hă-ZŌT?

92. Who is this man?

מִי הָאִישׁ הַזֶּה?

mee hă-EESH hă-ZĔ?

93. Who is this woman?

מִי הָאִשָּׁה הַזֹּאת?

mee hă-ee-SHĂ hă-ZŌT?

94. Where is [the men's room]?

אֵיפֹה [חֲדַר הַנּוֹחִיּוּת לִגְבָרִים]?

ay-FŌ [khă-DĂR hă-nŏ-khee-YOOT lee-g‿vă-REEM]?

95. ——— ladies' room.

חֲדַר הַנּוֹחִיּוּת לְנָשִׁים.

khă-DĂR hă-nŏ-khee-YOOT l‿nă-SHEEM.

96. ——— the bathroom.

חֲדַר הָאַמְבַּטְיָה.

khă-DĂR hă-ăm-BĂT-yă.

97. Where can I wash?

אֵיפֹה אוּכַל לְהִתְרַחֵץ?

ay-FŌ oo-KHĂL l‿heet-ră-KHĔTS?

98. Why?

מַדּוּעַ?

mă-DOO-ă?

99. How?

אֵיךְ?

aykh?

100. What for?

לָמָּה?

LĂ-mă?

101. What do you want?

מָה (אַתָּה רוֹצֶה) (אַתְּ רוֹצָה)?

mă (ă-TĂ rŏ-TSĔ TO M.) (ăt rŏ-TSĂ TO F.)?

102. Come here.

(בֹּא) (בֹּאִי) הֵנָּה.

(bŏ TO M.) (BŎ-ee TO F.) HĔ-nă.

103. Come in.

(הִכָּנֵס) (הִכָּנְסִי).

(hee-kă-NĔS TO M.) (hee-kă-N‿SEE TO F.).

104. Wait a moment.

(חַכֵּה) (חַכִּי) רֶגַע.

(khă-KĔ TO M.) (khă-KEE TO F.) RĔ-ga.

105. Not yet.

עוֹד לֹא.

ŏd lŏ.

106. Not now.

לֹא עַכְשָׁו.

lŏ ăkh-SHĂV.

107. Listen.

(שְׁמַע) (שִׁמְעִי).

(sh‿mă TO M.) (shee-M‿EE TO F.).

108. Look out!

(הִזָּהֵר) (הִזָּהֲרִי)!

(hee-ză-HĔR TO M.) (hee-ză-hă-REE TO F.)!

DIFFICULTIES AND REPAIRS

109. Can you help me?

הַאִם (תּוּכַל) (תּוּכְלִי) לַעֲזוֹר לִי?

hă-EEM (too-KHĂL TO M.) (too-KH‿LEE TO F.) lă-ă-ZŎR lee?

110. Can you tell me?

הַאִם (תּוּכַל) (תּוּכְלִי) לוֹמַר לִי?

hă-EEM (too-KHĂL TO M.) (too-KH‿LEE TO F.) lŏ-MĂR lee?

111. I am looking for my [friends].

אֲנִי (מְחַפֵּשׂ) (מְחַפֶּשֶׂת) אֶת [(הַחֲבֵרִים) (הַחֲבֵרוֹת)] שֶׁלִּי.

ă-NEE (m‿khă-PĔS M.) (m‿khă-PĔ-sĕt F.) ĕt [(hă-khă-vĕ-REEM M.) (hă-khă-vĕ-RŎT F.)] shĕ-LEE.

112. I cannot find my hotel address.

אֵינֶנִּי (יָכוֹל) (יְכוֹלָה) לִמְצֹא אֶת כְּתֹבֶת הַמָּלוֹן שֶׁלִּי.

ay-NĔ-nee (yă-KHŎL M.) (y‿khŏ-LĂ F.) leem-TSŎ ĕt K‿TŎ-vĕt hă-mă-LŎN shĕ-LEE.

113. I lost [my purse] .

אָבַד לִי [הָאַרְנָק].

ă-VĂD lee [hă-ăr-NĂK].

114. He forgot [his money].

הוּא שָׁכַח [אֶת הַכֶּסֶף].

hoo shă-KHĂKH [ĕt hă-KĔ-sĕf].

115. What is it? What's happened?

מַה יֵשׁ? מַה קָרָה?

mă yĕsh? mă kă-RĂ?

116. What shall I do?

מַה לַעֲשׂוֹת עַכְשָׁו?

mă lă-ă-SŌT ăkh-SHĂV?

117. [My eyeglasses] are broken.

[הַמִּשְׁקָפַיִם שֶׁלִּי] שְׁבוּרִים.

[hă-meesh-kă-FĂ-yeem shĕ-LEE] sh⌣voo-REEM.

118. Ask at [the lost-and-found office].

(שְׁאַל) (שַׁאֲלִי) [בְּמִשְׂרַד אֲבֵדוֹת וּמְצִיאוֹת].

(sh⌣ăl TO M.*) (shă-ă-LEE* TO F.*) [b⌣mees-RĂD ă-vĕ-DŌT oo-m⌣tsee-ŌT].*

119. ——— the police station.

בְּתַחֲנַת הַמִּשְׁטָרָה.

b⌣tă-khă-NĂT hă-meesh-tă-RĂ.

120. I will call [the policeman].

אֲנִי אֶקְרָא [לַשּׁוֹטֵר].

ă-NEE ĕk-RĂ [lă-shŏ-TĔR].

121. I will telephone the American consulate.

אֲנִי אֲטַלְפֵּן לַקּוֹנְסוּלְיָה הָאֲמֵרִיקָנִית.

ă-NEE ă-tăl-PĔN lă-kŏn-SOOL-yă hă-ă-mĕ-ree-kă-NEET.

CUSTOMS

122. Where is [the customs house] ?

אֵיפֹה [בֵּית־הַמֶּכֶס]?

ay-FŌ [bayt hă-MĔ-khĕs]?

123. Here is [my baggage].

הִנֵּה [הַמִּטְעָן שֶׁלִּי].

hee-NĔ [hă-meet-ĂN shĕ-LEE].

124. ——— my passport.

הַדַּרְכּוֹן שֶׁלִּי.

hă-dăr-KŌN shĕ-LEE.

125. ——— my identification card.

תְּעוּדַת הַזֶּהוּת שֶׁלִּי.

t⌣oo-DĂT hă-zĕ-HOOT shĕ-LEE.

126. ——— my health certificate.

תְּעוּדַת הַבְּרִיאוּת שֶׁלִּי.

t⌣oo-DĂT hă-b⌣ree-OOT shĕ-LEE.

127. ——— my visitor's visa.

אַשְׁרַת הַבִּקּוּר שֶׁלִּי.

ăsh-RĂT hă-bee-KOOR shĕ-LEE.

128. [These bags] are mine.

[הַחֲפָצִים הָאֵלֶּה] הֵם שֶׁלִּי.

[hă-khă-fā-TSEEM hă-Ĕ-lĕ] hĕm shĕ-LEE.

129. I have nothing to declare.

אֵין לִי עַל מַה לְהַצְהִיר.

ayn lee ăl mă l‿hăts-HEER.

130. All this is for my personal use.

כָּל זֶה לַשִּׁמּוּשׁ הַפְּרָטִי שֶׁלִּי.

kŏl zĕ lă-shee-MOOSH hă-p‿ră-TEE shĕ-LEE.

131. Is it necessary to open everything?

הַאִם צָרִיךְ לִפְתּוֹחַ הַכֹּל?

hă-EEM tsă-REEKH leef-TŎ-ăkh hă-KŎL?

132. I cannot open the trunk.

אֵינֶנִּי (יָכוֹל) (יְכוֹלָה) לִפְתּוֹחַ אֶת הָאַרְגָּז.

ay-NĔ-nee (yă-KHŎL m.) (y‿khŏ-LĂ f.) leef-TŎ-ăkh ĕt hă-ăr-GĂZ.

133. There is nothing here but clothing.

חוּץ מִבְּגָדִים אֵין כָּאן כְּלוּם.

khoots mee-b‿gă-DEEM ayn kăn kloom.

134. These are gifts.

אֵלֶּה מַתָּנוֹת.

Ĕ-lĕ mă-tă-NŎT.

135. Must duty be paid on these things?

הַאִם צָרִיךְ לְשַׁלֵּם מֶכֶס בְּעַד הַדְּבָרִים הָאֵלֶּה?

hă-EEM tsă-REEKH l‿shă-LĔM MĔ-khĕs b‿ăd hă-d‿vă-REEM hă-Ĕ-lĕ?

136. How much must I pay?

כַּמָּה עָלַי לְשַׁלֵּם?

kă-MĂ ă-LĪ l‿shă-LĔM?

137. That is all I have.

זֶה כָּל מַה שֶׁיֵּשׁ לִי.

zĕ kŏl mă shĕ-YĔSH lee.

138. Have you finished?

הַאִם (גָּמַרְתָּ) (גָּמַרְתְּ)?

hă-EEM (gă-MĂR-tă to m.) (gă-MĂRT to f.)?

BAGGAGE

139. Where can we check baggage through [to Tel Aviv]?

אֵיךְ נוּכַל לְהַעֲבִיר אֶת הַמִּטְעָן [לְתֵל־אָבִיב]?

aykh noo-KHĂL l‿hă-ă-VEER ĕt hă-meet-ĂN [l‿tĕl ă-VEEV]?

140. The baggage room.

חֲדַר הַמִּטְעָן.

khă-DĂR hă-meet-ĂN.

141. I want to leave these packages here for a few hours.

אֲנִי (רוֹצֶה) (רוֹצָה) לְהַשְׁאִיר כָּאן אֶת הַחֲבִילוֹת הָאֵלֶּה לְשָׁעוֹת אֲחָדוֹת.

ă-NEE (rŏ-TSĚ M.) *(rŏ-TSĂ* F.) *l⌣hăsh-EER kän ĕt hă-khă-vee-LŌT hă-Ě-lĕ l⌣shă-ŌT ă-khă-DŌT.*

142. Handle this very carefully.

(טַפֵּל) (טַפְּלִי) בְּזֶה בִּזְהִירוּת רַבָּה.

(tă-PĚL TO M.) *(tăp-LEE* TO F.) *bă-ZĚ bee-z⌣hee-ROOT ră-BĂ.*

TRAVEL DIRECTIONS

143. I want to go [to the airline office].

אֲנִי (רוֹצֶה) (רוֹצָה) לָלֶכֶת [לְמִשְׂרַד חֶבְרַת הַתְּעוּפָה].

ă-NEE (rŏ-TSĚ M.) *(rŏ-TSĂ* F.) *lă-LĚ-khĕt [l⌣mees-RĂD khĕv-RĂT hă-t⌣oo-FĂ].*

144. ———— to the travel agents' office.

לְמִשְׂרַד סוֹכְנוּת הַנְּסִיעוֹת.

l⌣mees-RĂD sŏ-KH⌣NOOT hă-n⌣see-ŌT.

145. ———— to the tourist office.

לְלִשְׁכַּת הַתַּיָּרוּת הַמֶּמְשַׁלְתִּית.

l⌣leesh-KĂT hă-tă-yă-ROOT hă-mĕm-shăl-TEET.

146. How long does it take to go [to Tiberias]?

כַּמָּה זְמַן נִמְשֶׁכֶת הַנְּסִיעָה [לִטְבֶרְיָה]?

kă-MĂ z⌣män neem-SHĚ-khĕt hă-n⌣see-Ă [lee-t⌣vĕr-YĂ]?

147. When will we arrive [at the Sea of Galilee]?

מָתַי נַגִּיעַ [לְיָם כִּנֶּרֶת]?

mă-TĬ nă-GEE-a [l⌣yăm kee-NĚ-rĕt]?

148. Is this the short way [to Haifa port]?

הַאִם זֹאת הַדֶּרֶךְ הַקְּצָרָה [לִנְמַל חֵיפָה]?

hă-EEM zŏt hă-DĚ-rĕkh hă-k⌣tsă-RĂ [lee-N⌣MĂL khay-FĂ]?

149. Please show me the way [to the business section].

(הַרְאֵה) (הַרְאִי) לִי, בְּבַקָּשָׁה, אֶת הַדֶּרֶךְ [לַמֶּרְכָּז הַמִּסְחָרִי].

(hăr-Ě TO M.) *(hăr-EE* TO F.) *lee, b⌣vă-kă-SHĂ, ĕt hă-DĚ-rĕkh [lă-mĕr-KĂZ hă-mees-khă-REE].*

150. ———— to the residential section.

לְרֹבַע הַמְּגוּרִים.

l⌣RŌ-vă hă-m⌣goo-REEM.

151. ———— to the city.

לָעִיר.

lă-EER.

152. —— to the village.
לַכְּפָר.
lă-K⌣FÁR.

153. Do I turn [to the north]?
הַאִם עָלַי לִפְנוֹת [צָפוֹנָה]?
hă-EEM ă-LÍ leef-NŎT [tsă-FŎ-nă]?

154. —— to the south.
דָּרוֹמָה.
dă-RŎ-mă.

155. —— to the east.
מִזְרָחָה.
meez-RÁ-khă.

156. —— to the west.
מַעֲרָבָה.
mă-ă-RÁ-vă.

157. —— to the right.
יָמִינָה.
yă-MEE-nă.

158. —— to the left.
שְׂמֹאלָה.
S⌣MŎ-lă.

159. Which [street] is this?
אֵיזֶה [רְחוֹב] זֶה?
AY-zě [r⌣khŏv] ză?

160. Where is it?
אֵיפֹה זֶה?
ay-FŎ ză?

161. How far is it?
מַה הַמֶּרְחָק לְשָׁם?
mă hă-měr-KHÁK l⌣shăm?

162. Can I walk there?
הַאִם אוּכַל לָלֶכֶת לְשָׁם בְּרַגְלִי?
hă-EEM oo-KHÁL lă-LĚ-khět l⌣shăm bă-RĚ-gěl?

163. Am I going in the right direction?
הַאִם אֲנִי (הוֹלֵךְ) (הוֹלֶכֶת) בַּכִּוּוּן הַנָּכוֹן?
hă-EEM ă-NEE (hŏ-LEKH M.) (hŏ-LĚ-khět F.) bă-kee-VOON
hă-nă-KHON?

164. Should I go [this way]?
הַאִם עָלַי לָלֶכֶת [בַּכִּוּוּן הַזֶּה]?
hă-EEM ă-LÍ lă-LĚ-khět [bă-kee-VOON hă-ZĚ]?

165. —— that way.
בַּכִּוּוּן הַהוּא.
bă-kee-VOON hă-HOO.

166. Is it [on this side of the street]?
הַאִם זֶה [בְּצַד זֶה שֶׁל הָרְחוֹב]?
hă-EEM ză [b⌣tsăd ză shěl hă-R⌣KHŎV]?

167. —— on the opposite side.
בַּצַד שֶׁמּוּל.
bă-TSÁD shě-mee-MOOL.

168. —— across the bridge.
מֵעֵבֶר לַגֶּשֶׁר.
mě-Ě-věr lă-GĚ-shěr.

169. ——— along the boulevard.
לְאֹרֶךְ הַשְׂדֵרָה.
L_Ŏ-rĕkh hă-sh_dĕ-RĂ.

170. ——— beyond the traffic light.
מֵאֲחוֹרֵי הָרַמְזוֹר.
mĕ-ă-khŏ-RAY hă-răm-ZŎR.

171. ——— at the corner.
בַּפִּנָּה.
bă-pee-NĂ.

172. ——— in the middle.
בָּאֶמְצַע.
bă-ĔM-tsă.

173. ——— back.
מֵאָחוֹר.
mĕ-ă-KHŎR.

174. ——— straight ahead.
יָשָׁר קָדִימָה.
yă-SHĂR kă-DEE-mă.

175. ——— at the entrance.
בַּכְּנִיסָה.
bă-k_nee-SĂ.

176. ——— opposite the park.
מוּל הַגַּן הַצִּבּוּרִי.
mool hă-GĂN hă-tsee-boo-REE.

177. ——— beside the school.
עַל־יַד בֵּית־הַסֵּפֶר.
ăl yăd bayt hă-SĔ-fĕr.

178. ——— up the hill.
בְּמַעֲלֵה הַגִּבְעָה.
b_mă-ă-LĔ hă-geev-Ă.

179. ——— down the road.
בְּמוֹרַד הַכְּבִישׁ.
b_mŏ-RĂD hă-K_VEESH.

180. Thanks for the help.
תּוֹדָה עַל הָעֶזְרָה.
tŏ-DĂ ăl hă-ĕz-RĂ.

TICKETS

181. Where is [the ticket window]?
אֵיפֹה [הַקֻּפָּה]?
ay-FO [hă-koo-PA]?

182. How much is a round-trip ticket [to Haifa]?
כַּמָּה עוֹלֶה כַּרְטִיס הָלוֹךְ וָשׁוֹב [לְחֵיפָה]?
kă-MĂ ŏ-LĔ kăr-TEES hă-LŎKH vă-SHŎV [l_khay-FĂ]?

183. A one-way ticket.
כַּרְטִיס לְכִוּוּן אֶחָד.
kăr-TEES l_khee-VOON ĕ-KHĂD.

184. Local train.
רַכֶּבֶת מְאַסֵּף.•
ră-KĔ-vĕt m_ă-SĔF.

185. Express train.
רַכֶּבֶת יְשִׁירָה.
ră-KĔ-vĕt y_shee-RĂ.

186. A reserved seat.
מָקוֹם שָׁמוּר.
mă-KŎM shă-MOOR.

187. The waiting room.
חֲדַר הַמְתָּנָה.
khă-DĂR hăm-tă-NĂ.

• Should be מְאַסֶּפֶת (m_ă-SĔ-fĕt).

188. May I stop [at Netanya] on the way?

הַאִם אוּכַל לְהִתְעַכֵּב בַּדֶּרֶךְ [בִּנְתַנְיָה]?

hă-EEM oo-KHĂL l⸺heet-ă-KĔV bă-DĔ-rĕkh [bee-N⸺TĂN-yă]?

BOAT

189. When must I go on board?

מָתַי עָלַי לַעֲלוֹת עַל הָאֳנִיָּה?

mă-TĪ ă-LĪ lă-ă-LŌT ăl hă-ŏ-nee-YĂ?

190. Bon voyage!

דֶּרֶךְ צְלֵחָה!

DĔ-rĕkh ts⸺lĕ-KHĂ!

191. Where is [the steward]?

אֵיפֹה [הַמֶּלְצַר]?

ay-FŌ [hă-mĕl-TSĂR]?

192. ⸺⸺⸺ the purser.

הַגִּזְבָּר.

hă-geez-BĂR.

193. ⸺⸺⸺ the captain.

רַב־הַחוֹבֵל.

răv hă-khŏ-VĔL.

194. ⸺⸺⸺ the dock.

הָרָצִיף.

hă-ră-TSEEF.

195. ⸺⸺⸺ the cabin.

הַתָּא.

hă-TĂ.

196. ⸺⸺⸺ the deck.

הַסִּפּוּן.

hă-see-POON.

AIRPLANE

197. I want to make a plane reservation.

אֲנִי (רוֹצֶה) (רוֹצָה) לְהַזְמִין מָקוֹם בְּמָטוֹס.

ă-NEE (ro-TSĔ m.) (rŏ-TSĂ f.) l⸺hăz-MEEN mă-KŌM b⸺mă-TŌS.

198. First class.

מַחְלָקָה רִאשׁוֹנָה.

măkh-lă-KĂ ree-shŏ-NĂ.

199. Second class.

מַחְלָקָה שְׁנִיָּה.

măkh-lă-KĂ sh⸺nee-YĂ.

200. I want to confirm the reservation.

אֲנִי (רוֹצֶה) (רוֹצָה) לְאַשֵּׁר אֶת הַהַזְמָנָה.*

ă-NEE (rŏ-TSĔ m.) (rŏ-TSĂ f.) l⸺ă-SHĔR ĕt hă-hăz-mă-NĂ.

201. Is there [bus service] between the hotel and the airport?

הַאִם יֵשׁ [שֵׁרוּת אוֹטוֹבּוּסִים] בֵּין הַמָּלוֹן לִשְׂדֵה הַתְּעוּפָה?

hă-EEM yĕsh [shĕ-ROOT ŏ-tŏ-boo-SEEM] bayn hă-mă-LŌN lee-S⸺DĔ hă-t⸺oo-FĂ?

202. At what time will they call for me?

בְּאֵיזוֹ שָׁעָה יָבוֹאוּ לָקַחַת אוֹתִי?

b⸺ay-ZŌ shă-Ă yă-VŌ-oo lă-KĂ-khăt ŏ-TEE?

---

* A more correct word for "confirm" is לְוַדֵּא (*l⸺vă-DĔ*).

203. Is flight twenty-three on time?

הַאִם טִיסָה מִסְפָּר עֶשְׂרִים וְשָׁלוֹשׁ מַגִּיעָה בַּזְּמָן?

hă-EEM tee-SĂ mees-PĂR ĕs-REEM ṿ-shă-LŎSH mă-gee-Ă bă-Z̧MĂN?

204. How many kilos may I take?

כַּמָּה קִילוֹגְרָם אוּכַל לָקַחַת אִתִּי?

kă-MĂ kee-lŏ-GRĂM oo-KHĂL lă-KĂ-khăt ee-TEE?

205. How much per kilo for excess baggage?

כַּמָּה דוֹרְשִׁים בְּעַד כָּל קִילוֹגְרָם שֶׁל מִטְעָן עוֹדֵף?

kă-MĂ dŏ-ŖSHEEM ḅ-ăd kŏl kee-lŏ-GRĂM shĕl meet-ĂN ŏ-DĔF?

TRAIN

206. Where is [the railroad station]?

אֵיפֹה [תַּחֲנַת הָרַכֶּבֶת]?

ay-FŎ [tă-khă-NĂT hă-ră-KĔ-vĕt]?

207. When does [the train] for Jerusalem leave?

מָתַי יוֹצֵאת [הָרַכֶּבֶת] לִירוּשָׁלַיִם?

mă-TĪ yŏ-TSĔT [hă-ră-KĔ-vĕt] lee-roo-shă-LĂ-yeem?

208. From which track does the train leave?

מֵאֵיזֶה רָצִיף יוֹצֵאת הָרַכֶּבֶת?

mĕ-ay-ZĔ ră-TSEEF yŏ-TSĔT hă-ră-KĔ-vĕt?

209. Open the window, please.

(פְּתַח) (פִּתְחִי) אֶת הַחַלּוֹן, בְּבַקָּשָׁה.

(p̧-tăkh TO M.) *(pee-Ţ-KHEE* TO F.) *ĕt hă-khă-LŎN, ḅ-vă-kă-SHĂ.*

210. Close the door.

(סְגֹר) (סִגְרִי) אֶת הַדֶּלֶת.

(ş-gŏr TO M.) *(see-Ģ-REE* TO F.) *ĕt hă-DĔ-lĕt.*

211. Where is [the diner]?

אֵיפֹה [קְרוֹן הַמִּזְנוֹן]?

ay-FŎ [ķ-rŏn hă-meez-NŎN]?

212. Where are we now?

אֵיפֹה אֲנַחְנוּ עַכְשָׁו?

ay-FŎ ă-NĂKH-noo ăkh-SHĂV?

213. May I smoke here?

הַאִם אוּכַל לְעַשֵּׁן פֹּה?

hă-EEM oo-KHĂL ļ-ă-SHEN pŏ?

BUS, STREETCAR AND SUBWAY

214. Which bus goes [to Dizengoff Square]?

אֵיזֶה אוֹטוֹבּוּס נוֹסֵעַ [לְכִכָּר דִּיזֶנְגּוֹף]?

ay-ZĚ ŏ-tŏ-BOOS nŏ-SĚ-ă [l⌣khee-KĂR DEE-zĕn-gŏf]?

215. Where is [the bus stop]?

אֵיפֹה [תַּחֲנַת הָאוֹטוֹבּוּסִים]?

ay-FÓ [tă-khă-NĂT hă-ŏ-tŏ-boo-SEEM]?

216. Does the subway stop near [the Technion]?

הַאִם הָרַכֶּבֶת הַתַּחְתִּית נֶעֱצֶרֶת עַל־יַד [הַטֶּכְנִיּוֹן]?

hă-EEM hă-ră-KĚ-vĕt hă-tăkh-TEET nĕ-ĕ-TSĚ-rĕt ăl yăd [hă-tĕkh-nee-YÓN]?

217. A token, please.

אֲסִימוֹן, בְּבַקָּשָׁה.

ă-see-MÓN, b⌣vă-kă-SHĂ.

218. Driver, please tell me where to get off.

נֶהָג, אֱמֹר לִי בְּבַקָּשָׁה אֵיפֹה לָרֶדֶת.

nĕ-HĂG, ĕ-MÓR lee b⌣vă-kă-SHĂ ay-FÓ lă-RĚ-dĕt.

TAXI

219. Please call a taxi for me.

(הַזְמֵן) לִי מוֹנִית, בְּבַקָּשָׁה.

(hăz-MĚN TO M.) lee mŏ-NEET, b⌣vă-kă-SHĂ.

220. Are you free?

הַאִם (אַתָּה פָּנוּי)?

hă-EEM (ă-TĂ pă-NOOEY TO M.)?

221. How much do you charge per hour?

מַה הַמְּחִיר לְשָׁעָה?

mă hă-M⌣KHEER l⌣shă-Ă?

222. —— per kilometer.

לְקִילוֹמֶטֶר.

l⌣kee-lŏ-MĚ-ter.

223. Please drive more slowly.

(סַע) יוֹתֵר לְאַט בְּבַקָּשָׁה.

(să TO M.) yŏ-TĔR l⌣ăt b⌣vă-kă-SHĂ.

224. Stop here.

(עֲצֹר) כָּאן.

(ă-TSÓR TO M.) kăn.

225. Wait for me.

(חַכֵּה) לִי.

(khă-KĚ to M.) lee.

AUTOMOBILE TRAVEL

226. Where can I rent [a car]?

אֵיפֹה אוּכַל לִשְׂכֹּר [מְכוֹנִית]?

ay-FÓ oo-KHÁL lees-KÓR [m‿khŏ-NEET]?

227. I have [an international driver's license].

יֵשׁ לִי [רִשְׁיוֹן נְהִיגָה בֵּינְלְאֻמִּי].

yĕsh lee [reesh-YÓN n‿hee-GÁ bayn-l‿oo-MEE].

228. A gas station.

תַּחֲנַת דֶּלֶק.

tă-khă-NÁT DÉ-lĕk.

229. A garage.

מוּסָךְ.

moo-SÁKH.

230. A mechanic.

מְכוֹנַאי.

m‿khŏ-NÍ.

231. Is the road [good]?

הַאִם הַכְּבִישׁ [טוֹב]?

hă-EEM hă-K‿VEESH [tŏv]?

232. —— bad.

גָּרוּעַ.

gă-ROO-ă.

233. Where does [this road] lead to?

לְאָן מוֹבִיל [הַכְּבִישׁ הַזֶּה]?

l‿ăn mŏ-VEEL [hă-K‿VEESH hă-ZÉ]?

234. [What town] is this?

[אֵיזוֹ עִיר] הִיא זֹאת?

[ay-ZÓ eer] hee zŏt?

235. What is the distance [to the next settlement]?

מַה הַמֶּרְחָק [לַנְּקוּדָה הַקְּרוֹבָה]?

mă hă-mĕr-KHÁK [lă-n‿koo-DÁ hă-k‿rŏ-VÁ]?

236. Can you show it to me [on the road map]?

הַאִם תּוּכַל לְהַרְאוֹת לִי אוֹתָהּ [עַל מַפַּת הַדְּרָכִים]?

hă-EEM too-KHÁL l‿hăr-ÓT lee ŏ-TÁ [ăl mă-PÁT hă-d‿ră-KHEEM]?

237. Give me [ten gallons].

תֵּן לִי [עֲשָׂרָה גָּלוֹן].

tĕn lee [ă-să-RÁ gă-LÓN].

238. Check the oil, please.

בְּדֹק אֶת הַשֶּׁמֶן, בְּבַקָּשָׁה.

b‿dŏk ĕt hă-SHÉ-mĕn, b‿vă-kă-SHÁ.

239. Fill the radiator.

מַלֵּא אֶת הָרַדְיָטוֹר.

mă-LÉ ĕt hă-răd-YÁ-tŏr.

240. Lubricate the car.

שַׁמֵּן אֶת הַמְּכוֹנִית.

shă-MÉN ĕt hă-m‿khŏ-NEET.

241. Charge the battery.

הַטְעֵן אֶת הַסּוֹלְלָה.

hăt-ĔN ĕt hă-sŏ-L‿LĂ.

242. Adjust the brakes.

כַּוֵּן אֶת הַבְּלָמִים.

kăv-NĔN ĕt hă-b‿lă-MEEM.

243. Check the tires.

בְּדֹק אֶת הַצְּמִיגִים.

b‿dŏk ĕt hă-ts‿mee-GEEM.

244. Will you be able to repair [the flat tire] now?

הַאִם תּוּכַל לְתַקֵּן [אֶת הַתֶּקֶר] עַכְשָׁו

hă-EEM too-KHĂL l‿tă-KĔN [ĕt hă-TĔ-kĕr] ăkh-SHĂV?

245. It does not work properly.

הַמְּכוֹנִית אֵינֶנָּה פּוֹעֶלֶת כַּהֲלָכָה.

hă-m‿khŏ-NEET ay-NĔ-nă pŏ-Ĕ-lĕt kă-hă-lă-KHĂ.

246. The engine overheats.

הַמָּנוֹעַ מִתְחַמֵּם יוֹתֵר מִדַּי.

hă-mă-NŎ-ă meet-khă-MĔM yŏ-TĔR mee-DĪ.

247. The motor stalls.

הַמָּנוֹעַ מִזְדַּקֵּר.

hă-mă-NŎ-ă meez-dă-KĔR.

248. May I park here for a while?

הַאִם אוּכַל לַחֲנוֹת פֹּה זְמַן מָה?

hă-EEM oo-KHĂL lă-khă-NŎT pŏ z‿măn mă?

249. The lights do not work properly.

הָאוֹרוֹת אֵינָם פּוֹעֲלִים כַּהֲלָכָה.

hă-ŏ-RŎT ay-NĂM pŏ-ă-LEEM kă-hă-lă-KHĂ.

HOTEL AND APARTMENT

250. I am looking for [a good hotel].

אֲנִי (מְחַפֵּשׂ) (מְחַפֶּשֶׂת) [מָלוֹן טוֹב].

ă-NEE (m‿khă-PES m.) (m‿khă-PĔ-sĕt f.) [mă-LŎN tŏv].

251. —— an inexpensive hotel.

מָלוֹן לֹא יָקָר.

mă-LŎN lŏ yă-KĂR.

252. —— a boarding house.

פֶּנְסִיוֹן.

pĕn-S‿YŎN.

253. —— a furnished apartment.

דִּירָה מְרֻהֶטֶת.

dee-RĂ m‿roo-HĔ-lĕt.

18

254. I do not want to stay in the center of town.

אֵינֶנִּי (רוֹצֶה) (רוֹצָה) לָגוּר בְּמֶרְכַּז הָעִיר.

ay-NĚ-nee (ro-TSĚ M.) *(rŏ-TSĂ* F.) *lă-GOOR b⌣měr-KĂZ hă-EER.*

255. I prefer a quiet place.

אֲנִי (מַעֲדִיף) (מַעֲדִיפָה) מָקוֹם שָׁקֵט.

ă-NEE (mă-ă-DEEF M.) *(mă-ă-dee-FĂ* F.) *mă-KŎM shă-KĚT.*

256. I have a reservation [for today].

יֵשׁ לִי הַזְמָנָה [לְהַיּוֹם].

yěsh lee hăz-mă-NĂ [l⌣hă-YŎM].

257. Do you have a vacant room?

הַאִם (יֵשׁ לָכֶם) חֶדֶר פָּנוּי?

hă-EEM (yěsh lă-KHĚM) (to M. PL.) *KHĚ-děr pă-NOOEY?*

258. A single room.

חֶדֶר בּוֹדֵד.

KHĚ-děr bŏ-DĚD.

259. A double room.

חֶדֶר כָּפוּל.

KHĚ-děr kă-FOOL.

260. An air-conditioned room.

חֶדֶר עִם מִזּוּג אֲוִיר.

KHĚ-děr eem mee-ZOOG ă-VEER.

261. A suite.

דִּירָה.

dee-RĂ.

262. A safe deposit box.

כַּסֶּפֶת.

kă-SĚ-fět.

263. I want a room with [a double bed].

אֲנִי (רוֹצֶה) (רוֹצָה) חֶדֶר עִם [מִטָּה כְּפוּלָה].

ă-NEE (rŏ-TSĚ M.) *(rŏ-TSĂ* F.) *KHĚ-děr eem [mee-TĂ k⌣foo-LĂ].*

264. —— twin beds.

שְׁתֵּי מִטּוֹת.

sh⌣tay mee-TŎT.

265. —— a bath.

חֲדַר אַמְבַּטְיָה.

khă-DAR ăm-BĂT-yă.

266. —— a shower.

מִקְלַחַת.

meek-LĂ-khăt.

267. I want a room [without meals].

אֲנִי (רוֹצֶה) (רוֹצָה) חֶדֶר [בְּלִי אֲרוּחוֹת].

ă-NEE (rŏ-TSĚ M.) *(rŏ-TSĂ* F.) *KHĚ-děr [b⌣lee ă-roo-KHŎT].*

268. ——— for tonight.

לְהַלַּיְלָה.

l˄hă-LI-lă.

269. ——— for several days.

לְיָמִים אֲחָדִים.

l˄yă-MEEM ă-khă-DEEM.

270. ——— for two persons.

לִשְׁנַיִם.

lee-SH˄NÅ-yeem.

271. I should like to see the room.

הָיִיתִי (רוֹצֶה) (רוֹצָה) לִרְאוֹת אֶת הַחֶדֶר.

hă-YEE-tee (rŏ-TSĔ m.) (rŏ-TSĂ f.) leer-ŎT ĕt hă-KHĔ-dĕr.

272. Is it [upstairs]?

הַאִם הוּא [לְמַעֲלָה]?

hă-EEM hoo [L˄MÅ-ă˄lă]?

273. ——— downstairs.

לְמַטָּה.

L˄MÅ-tă.

274. Is there [an elevator] here?

הַאִם יֵשׁ כָּאן [מַעֲלִית]?

hă-EEM yĕsh kăn [mă-ă-LEET]?

275. Service, please.

שֵׁרוּת, בְּבַקָּשָׁה.

shĕ-ROOT, b˄vă-kă-SHĂ.

276. Please send [a porter] to my room soon.

בְּבַקָּשָׁה לִשְׁלֹחַ מִיָּד [סַבָּל] לַחֶדֶר שֶׁלִּי.

b˄vă-kă-SHĂ leesh-LŎ-ăkh mee-YÅD [să-BÅL] lă-KHĔ-dĕr shĕ-LEE.

277. ——— a chambermaid.

חַדְרָנִית.

khăd-ră-NEET.

278. ——— a bellhop.

נַעַר מְשָׁרֵת.

NÅ-ăr m˄shă-RĔT.

279. Please wake me at [quarter past nine o'clock].

בְּבַקָּשָׁה לְהָעִיר אוֹתִי [בְּשָׁעָה תֵּשַׁע וָרֶבַע].

b˄vă-kă-SHĂ l˄hă-EER ŏ-TEE [b˄shă-Á TĔ-shă vă-RĔ-vă].

280. Please do not disturb me until then.

בְּבַקָּשָׁה לֹא לְהַפְרִיעַ לִי עַד אָז.

b˄vă-kă-SHĂ lŏ l˄hăf-REE-ă lee ăd ăz.

281. We should like to have breakfast [in our room].

הָיִינוּ רוֹצִים לֶאֱכֹל אֶת אֲרוּחַת-הַבֹּקֶר [בַּחֶדֶר].

hă-YEE-noo rŏ-TSEEM lĕ-ĕ-KHŎL ĕt ă-roo-KHĂT hă-BŎ-kĕr [bă-KHĔ-dĕr].

282. Who is it?

מִי שָׁם?

mee shăm?

20

283. Come back later.

.(שׁוּב) (שׁוּבִי) יוֹתֵר מְאֻחָר

(*shoov* TO M.) (*SHOO-vee* TO F.) *yŏ-TĔR m͟oo-KHĂR.*

284. I want [a blanket].

.[אֲנִי (רוֹצֶה) (רוֹצָה) [שְׂמִיכָה

ă-NEE (*rŏ-TSĔ* M.) (*rŏ-TSĂ* F.) [*s͟mee-KHĂ*].

285. ——— a pillow.

כַּר.

kăr.

286. ——— a pillowcase.

צִפִּיָה.

tsee-pee-YĂ.

287. ——— coat hangers.

קוֹלָבִים.

kŏ-lă-VEEM.

288. ——— sheets.

סְדִינִים.

s͟dee-NEEM.

289. ——— soap.

סַבּוֹן.

să-BŎN.

290. ——— towels.

מַגָּבוֹת.

mă-gă-VŎT.

291. ——— toilet paper.

נְיָר טוֹאָלֶט.

n͟yăr tŏ-ă-LĔT.

292. I should like to speak to the manager.

הָיִיתִי (רוֹצֶה) (רוֹצָה) לְדַבֵּר עִם הַמְנַהֵל.

hă-YEE-tee (*rŏ-TSĔ* M.) (*rŏ-TSĂ* F.) *l͟dă-BĔR eem hă-m͟nă-HĔL.*

293. My room key, please.

מַפְתֵּחַ הַחֶדֶר שֶׁלִּי, בְּבַקָּשָׁה.

măf-TĔ-ăkh hă-KHĔ-dĕr shĕ-LEE, b͟vă-kă-SHĂ.

294. Are there any letters or messages for me?

הַאִם יֵשׁ מִכְתָּבִים אוֹ הוֹדָעוֹת בִּשְׁבִילִי?

hă-EEM yĕsh meekh-tă-VEEM ŏ hŏ-dă-ŎT beesh-vee-LEE?

295. What is [my room number]?

מַה [מִסְפַּר הַחֶדֶר שֶׁלִּי]?

mă[mees-PĂR hă-KHĔ-dĕr shĕ-LEE]?

296. I am leaving the hotel at ten o'clock.

אֲנִי (עוֹזֵב) (עוֹזֶבֶת) אֶת הַמָּלוֹן בְּשָׁעָה עֶשֶׂר.

ă-NEE (*ŏ-ZĔV* M.) (*ŏ-ZĔ-vĕt* F.) *ĕt hă-mă-LŎN b͟shă-Ă Ĕ-sĕr.*

297. Please make out [my bill] as soon as possible.

בְּבַקָּשָׁה לְהָכִין [אֶת הַחֶשְׁבּוֹן שֶׁלִּי] בְּהֶקְדֵּם הָאֶפְשָׁרִי.

b͟vă-kă-SHĂ l͟hă-KHEEN [*ĕt hă-khĕsh-BŎN shĕ-LEE*] *bă-hĕk-DĔM hă-ĕf-shă-REE.*

298. Does this include [the service charge and tax]?

הַאִם זֶה כּוֹלֵל [דְּמֵי שֵׁרוּת וּמִסִּים]?

hă-EEM zĕ kŏ-LĔL [d⌣may shĕ-ROOT oo-mee-SEEM]?

299. Please forward my mail [to American Express in Jerusalem].

בְּבַקָּשָׁה לְהַעֲבִיר אֶת הַמִּכְתָּבִים שֶׁלִי [לְ «אָמֶרִיקֶן אֶכְּסְפְּרֶס»
בִּירוּשָׁלַיִם].

*b⌣vă-kă-SHĂ l⌣hă-ă-VEER ĕt hă-meekh-tă-VEEM shĕ-LEE [lă-
MĔ-ree-kĕn ĕks-PRĔS bee-roo-shă-LĂ-yeem].*

TELEPHONE CONVERSATION

300. בְּבַקָּשָׁה לְקַשֵּׁר אוֹתִי עִם שִׂיחוֹת חוּץ.

b⌣vă-kă-SHĂ l⌣kă-SHĔR ŏ-TEE eem see-KHŌT khoots.
Please connect me with Long Distance.

301. רֶגַע אֶחָד, בְּבַקָּשָׁה.

RĔ-gă ĕ-KHĂD, b⌣vă-kă-SHĂ.
One minute, please.

302. שִׂיחוֹת חוּץ.

see-KHŌT khoots.
Long Distance.

303. תְּנִי לִי בְּבַקָּשָׁה תֵּל־אָבִיב מִסְפָּר: אַחַת, שְׁתַּיִם, שָׁלוֹשׁ, אַרְבַּע, חָמֵשׁ.

*t⌣nee lee b⌣vă-kă-SHĂ TĔL ă-VEEV mees-PĂR: ă-KHĂT,
SH⌣TĂ-yeem, shă-LŌSH, ăr-BĂ, khă-MĔSH.*
Please give me Tel-Aviv 12345.

304. מִסְפָּרְךָ, אֲדוֹנִי?

mees-păr-KHĂ, ă-dŏ-NEE?
Your number, sir?

305. חֵיפָה, חָמֵשׁ, שֵׁשׁ, שֶׁבַע, שְׁמוֹנֶה, תֵּשַׁע. מַה הַמְּחִיר בְּעַד שָׁלוֹשׁ הַדַּקּוֹת
הָרִאשׁוֹנוֹת?

*khay-FĂ, khă-MĔSH, shĕsh, SHĔ-vă, SH⌣MŎ-nĕ, TĔ-shă. mă
hă-M⌣KHEER b⌣ăd shă-LŌSH hă-dă-KŌT hă-ree-shŏ-NŌT?*
Haifa, 56789. What is the charge for the first three minutes?

306. לִירָה וָחֵצִי. חַכֵּה בְּבַקָּשָׁה עַל הַקַּו. הִנֵּה הַשִּׂיחָה שֶׁלְּךָ.

*LEE-ră vă-KHĔ-tsee. khă-KĔ b⌣vă-kă-SHĂ ăl hă-KĂV. hee-
NĔ hă-see-KHĂ shĕl-KHĂ.*
IL 1·50. Hold the line please. Here is your party.

307. הַלוֹ. כָּאן מְדַבֵּר גֹ'ן וַיט. הַאִם אוּכַל לְדַבֵּר עִם דוֹקְטוֹר יוֹסֵף
לַנְדָאוּ?

*hă-LŎ. KÄN m⏑dă-BĚR "John White." hă-EEM oo-KHÄL
l⏑dă-BĚR eem DŎK-tŏr yŏ-SĚF "Landau"?*

Hello. This is John White speaking. May I speak to Dr.
Joseph Landau?

308. אֲנִי מִצְטָעֵר, אֵינֶי יְכוֹלָה לִשְׁמֹעַ אוֹתְךָ, הַקֶּשֶׁר חַלָּשׁ. הַאִם תּוּכַל
לְדַבֵּר בְּקוֹל רָם יוֹתֵר?

*ă-NEE meets-tă-Ě-rĕt, ay-NĚ-nee y⏑khŏ-LÄ leesh-MŎ-ă ŏ-
T⏑KHÄ, hă-KĚ-shĕr khă-LÄSH. hă-EEM too-KHÄL l⏑dă-
BĚR b⏑kŏl RÄM yŏ-TĚR?*

I'm sorry, I can't hear you. The connection is poor. Could
you speak a little louder?

309. מְדַבֵּר גֹ'ן וַיט. הָיִיתִי רוֹצֶה לְדַבֵּר עִם דוֹקְטוֹר לַנְדָאוּ.

*m⏑dă-BER "John White." hă-YEE-tee rŏ-TSĚ l⏑dă-BĚR eem
DŎK-tŏr "Landau."*

John White speaking. I'd like to speak with Dr. Landau.

310. אֲנִי מִצְטָעֵר, הוּא אֵינֶנּוּ בַּמִּשְׂרָד. הוּא לֹא יָשׁוּב לִפְנֵי תֵּשַׁע וָחֵצִי
בָּעֶרֶב.

*ă-NEE meets-tă-Ě-rĕt, hoo ay-NĚ-noo ba-mees-RÄD. hoo lŏ yă-
SHOOV leef-NAY TĚ-shă vă-KHĚ-tsee bă-Ě-rĕv.*

I'm sorry, he is not in the office. He won't be back before
9:30 this evening.

311. הַאִם אוּכַל לְהַשְׁאִיר לוֹ הוֹדָעָה? מִסְרִי לוֹ בְּבַקָּשָׁה שֶׁגֹ'ן וַיט טִלְפֵּן.
אֶהְיֶה בְּתֵל־אָבִיב בְּיוֹם רִאשׁוֹן. אֲנִי מְבַקֵּשׁ שֶׁיִּקְשֵׁר אִתִּי
בְּיוֹם רִאשׁוֹן בַּבֹּקֶר, לִפְנֵי עֶשֶׂר. אֲנִי נִמְצָא בְּמָלוֹן דָּן, חֶדֶר
שְׁלוֹשִׁים וּשְׁתַּיִם.

*hă-EEM oo-KHÄL l⏑hăsh-EER lŏ hŏ-dă-Ä? mees-REE lŏ b⏑vă-
kă-SHÄ shĕ-"John White" teel-PĚN. ĕh-YĚ b⏑tĕl ă-VEEV
b⏑yŏm ree-SHŎN. ă-NEE m⏑vă-KĚSH shĕ-yeet-kă-SHĚR ee-
TEE b⏑yŏm ree-SHŎN bă-BŎ-kĕr lee-F⏑NAY Ě-sĕr? ă-NEE
neem-TSÄ b⏑mă-LŎN dän, KHĚ-dĕr sh⏑lŏ-SHEEM oo-
SH⏑TÄ-yeem.*

May I leave a message for him? Will you tell him John White
called? I will be in Tel Aviv on Sunday. Will he please
call me Sunday morning before 10:00? I am stopping at
the Dan Hotel, Room 32.

312. רֶגַע אֶחָד, בְּבַקָּשָׁה. אֲנִי רוֹשֶׁמֶת אֶת זֶה. מָלוֹן דָּן. אָמַרְתָּ חֶדֶר
חֲמִשִּׁים וּשְׁתַּיִם?

*RĚ-gă ĕ-KHÄD, b⏑vă-kă-SHÄ. ă-NEE rŏ-SHĚ-mĕt ĕt zĕ. mă-
LŎN dän. ă-MÄR-tă KHĚ-dĕr khă-mee-SHEEM oo-SH⏑TÄ-
yeem?*

One minute, please. I will put this down. Dan Hotel.
Did you say Room 52?

313. לֹא, לֹא, חֶדֶר שְׁלֹשִׁים וּשְׁתַּיִם . . . סְלִיחָה עַל הַטִּרְחָה.

lŏ-lŏ-lŏ-lŏ, KHĔ-dĕr shŭ-lŏ-SHEEM oo-SHŭ-TÁ-yeem. . . . sⵧlee-
KHÁ äl ha-teer-KHÁ.

No, no, Room 32. . . . I'm sorry to have bothered you.

314. עַל לֹא דָּבָר. אֲנִי אֶדְאַג לְכַךְ שֶׁדּוֹקְטוֹר לַנְדָּאוּ יְקַבֵּל אֶת הַהוֹדָעָה.

äl lŏ dä-VÁR. ĕd-ÁG lⵧkhäkh shĕ-DÓK-tŏr Landau yⵧkä-BÉL ĕt
hä-hŏ-dä-Á.

Not at all. I'll see that Dr. Landau gets the message.

315. תּוֹדָה רַבָּה, שָׁלוֹם.

tŏ-DÁ rä-BÁ, shä-LÓM.

Thanks very much, goodbye.

316. שָׁלוֹם.

shä-LÓM.

Goodbye.

AT THE CAFÉ

317. I'd like to have [something to drink].

הָיִיתִי (רוֹצֶה) (רוֹצָה) לְקַבֵּל [מַשֶּׁהוּ לִשְׁתּוֹת].

hä-YEE-tee (rŏ-TSĔ M.) (rŏ-TSÁ F.) lⵧkä-BÉL [MÁ-shĕ-hoo
leesh-TÓT].

318. A bottle of soda water.

בַּקְבּוּק מֵי סוֹדָה.

bäk-BOOK may SÓ-dä.

319. A glass of sherry.

כּוֹסִית שֶׁרִי.

kŏ-SEET SHĔ-ree.

320. A non-alcoholic drink.

מַשְׁקֶה לֹא־חָרִיף.

mäsh-KĔ lŏ khä-REEF.

321. Light beer.

בִּירָה רְגִילָה.

BEE-rä rⵧgee-LÁ.

322. Dark beer.

בִּירָה שְׁחוֹרָה.

BEE-rä shⵧkhŏ-RÁ.

323. White wine.

יַיִן לָבָן.

YÁ-yeen lä-VÁN.

324. Red wine.

יַיִן אָדֹם.

YÁ-yeen ä-DÓM.

325. Let's have another.

נִשְׁתֶּה עוֹד כּוֹסִית.

neesh-TĔ ŏd kŏ-SEET.

326. To your health!

לְחַיִּים!

lⵧkha-YEEM!

AT THE RESTAURANT

327. Can you recommend a restaurant [for supper]?

הַאִם (תּוּכַל) (תּוּכְלִי) לְהַמְלִיץ עַל מִסְעָדָה [לַאֲרוּחַת־עֶרֶב]?

hä-EEM (too-KHÁL TO M.) (too-KHⵧLEE TO F.) lⵧhäm-LEETS
äl mees-ä-DÁ lä-ä-roo-KHÁT Ĕ-rĕv?

328. —— for breakfast.

לַאֲרוּחַת־בֹּקֶר.

lă-ă-roo-KHĂT BŎ-kĕr.

329. —— for dinner.

לַאֲרוּחַת צָהֳרַיִם.

lă-ă-roo-KHĂT tsŏ-hŏ-RĂ-yeem.

330. —— for a light meal.

לַאֲרוּחָה קַלָּה.

lă-ă-roo-KHĂ kă-LĂ.

331. At what time is [supper] served here?

בְּאֵיזוֹ שָׁעָה מַגִּשִׁים כָּאן [אֲרוּחַת־עֶרֶב]?

b⌣ay-ZŎ shă-Ă mă-gee-SHEEM kän [ă-roo-KHĂT Ĕ-rĕv]?

332. Are you serving my table?

הַאִם (אַתָּה מַגִּישׁ) (אַתְּ מַגִּישָׁה) לְשֻׁלְחָנִי?

hă-EEM (ă-TĂ mă-GEESH TO M.) (at mă-gee-SHĂ TO F.) l⌣shool- khă-NEE?

333. Are you the [headwaiter]?

הַאִם אַתָּה [הַמֶּלְצָר הָרָאשִׁי]?

hă-EEM ă-TĂ [hă-mĕl-TSĂR hă-ră-SHEE]?

334. Waitress!

מֶלְצָרִית!

mĕl-tsă-REET!

335. I should like a table for two by the window, if possible.

הָיִיתִי (רוֹצֶה) (רוֹצָה) שֻׁלְחָן לִשְׁנַיִם, עַל־יַד הַחַלּוֹן, אִם אֶפְשָׁר.

hă-YEE-tee (rŏ-TSĔ M.) (rŏ-TSĂ F.) shool-KHĂN lee-SH⌣NĂ-yeem, ăl yăd hă-khă-LŌN, eem ĕf-SHĂR.

336. [The menu], please.

[הַתַּפְרִיט] בְּבַקָּשָׁה.

[hă-tăf-REET] b⌣vă-kă-SHĂ.

337. The wine list.

רְשִׁימַת הַיֵּינוֹת.

r⌣shee-MĂT hă-yay-NŌT.

338. A napkin.

מַפִּית.

mă-PEET.

339. A fork.

מַזְלֵג.

măz-LĔG.

340. A knife.

סַכִּין.

să-KEEN.

341. A plate.

צַלַּחַת.

tsă-LĂ-khăt.

342. A teaspoon.

כַּפִּית.

kă-PEET.

343. A large spoon.

כַּף.

kăf.

344. I want to eat something light.

אֲנִי (רוֹצֶה) (רוֹצָה) לֶאֱכֹל מַשֶּׁהוּ קַל.

ă-NEE (rŏ-TSĔ m.) (rŏ-TSĂ f.) lĕ-ĕ-KHŎL MĂ-shĕ-hoo kăl.

345. Not too spicy.

לֹא חָרִיף מִדַּי.

lŏ khă-REEF mee-DĬ.

346. Not too sweet.

לֹא מָתוֹק מִדַּי.

lŏ mă-TŎK mee-DĬ.

347. Not too fat.

לֹא שָׁמֵן מִדַּי.

lŏ shă-MĔN mee-DĬ.

348. Fried.

מְטֻגָּן.

m‿too-GĂN.

349. Boiled.

מְבֻשָּׁל.

m‿voo-SHĂL.

350. I like the meat [rare].

אֲנִי אוֹהֵב אֶת הַבָּשָׂר [נָא].

ă-NEE ŏ-HĔV ĕt hă-bă-SĂR [nă].

351. —— well done.

עָשׂוּי הֵיטֵב.

ă-SOOEY hay-TĔV.

352. I did not order this.

לֹא הִזְמַנְתִּי אֶת זֶה.

lŏ heez-MĂN-tee ĕt zĕ.

353. Could I get [a salad] instead of this?

הַאִם אוּכַל לְקַבֵּל [סָלָט] בִּמְקוֹם זֶה?

hă-EEM oo-KHĂL l‿kă-BĔL [să-LĂT] bee-M‿KŎM zĕ?

354. The check, please.

הַחֶשְׁבּוֹן, בְּבַקָּשָׁה.

hă-khĕsh-BŎN, b‿vă-kă-SHĂ.

355. Does this include [the service charge]?

הַאִם זֶה כּוֹלֵל [אֶת דְּמֵי הַשֵּׁרוּת]?

hă-EEM zĕ kŏ-LĔL [ĕt d‿may hă-shĕ-ROOT]?

356. There is a mistake in the bill.

יֵשׁ טָעוּת בַּחֶשְׁבּוֹן.

yĕsh tă-OOT bă-khĕsh-BŎN.

357. What are these amounts for?

בְּעַד מָה הַסְּכוּמִים הָאֵלֶּה?

b‿ăd mă hă-s‿khoo-MEEM hă-Ĕ-lĕ?

358. Keep the change.

הָעֹדֶף (בִּשְׁבִילְךָ) (בִּשְׁבִילֵךְ).

hă-Ŏ-dĕf (beesh-veel-KHĂ to m.) (bee-sh‿vee-LĔKH to f.).

359. The food and service were excellent.

הָאֹכֶל וְהַשֵּׁרוּת הָיוּ מְצֻיָּנִים.

hă-Ŏ-khĕl v‿hă-shĕ-ROOT hă-YOO m‿tsoo-yă-NEEM.

360. Hearty appetite!

בְּתֵאָבוֹן!

bᴗtĕ-ă-VON!

361. Please bring me some water [with ice].

(הָבֵא) (הָבִיאִי) לִי בְּבַקָּשָׁה קְצָת מַיִם [בְּקֶרַח].

(*hă-VĔ* ᴛᴏ ᴍ.) (*hă-VEE-ee* ᴛᴏ ꜰ.) *lee bᴗvă-kă-SHĂ kᴗtsăt MĂ-yeem* [*BᴗKĔ-răkh*].

362. ——— without ice.

בְּלִי קֶרַח.

bᴗlee KĔ-răkh.

FOOD

363. Please pass the bread.

(הַעֲבֵר) (הַעֲבִירִי) בְּבַקָּשָׁה אֶת הַלֶּחֶם.

(*hă-ă-VĔR* ᴛᴏ ᴍ.) (*hă-ă-VEE-ree* ᴛᴏ ꜰ.) *bᴗvă-kă-SHĂ ĕt hă-LĔ- khĕm.*

364. Rolls.

לַחְמָנִיּוֹת.

lăkh-mă-nee-YŎT.

365. Butter.

חֶמְאָה.

khĕm-Ă.

366. Sugar.

סֻכָּר.

soo-KĂR.

367. Salt.

מֶלַח.

MĔ-lăkh.

368. Pepper.

פִּלְפֵּל.

peel-PĔL.

369. Oil.

שֶׁמֶן.

SHĔ-mĕn.

370. Vinegar.

חֹמֶץ.

KHŎ-mets.

371. Garlic.

שׁוּם.

shoom.

372. Catsup.

רֹטֶב עַגְבָנִיּוֹת.

RŎ-tĕv ăg-vă-nee-YŎT

373. Mustard.

חַרְדָּל.

khăr-DĂL.

374. Mayonnaise.

מָיוֹנִית.

mă-yŏ-NEET.

BREAKFAST FOODS

375. May I have [some fruit juice]?

הַאִם אוּכַל לְקַבֵּל [מִיץ פֵּרוֹת]?

hă-EEM oo-KHĂL lᴗkă-BĔL [*meets pĕ-RŎT*]?

376. ——— orange juice.

מִיץ תַּפּוּזִים.

meets tă-poo-ZEEM.

377. ——— tomato juice.

מִיץ עַגְבָנִיּוֹת.

meets ăg-vă-nee-YŎT.

378. ——— cereal.

דִּיסָה.

dī-SĂ.

379. ——— toast and jam.

לֶחֶם קָלוּי וְרִבָּה.

LĔ-khĕm kă-LOOEY v⌣ree-BĂ.

380. ——— an omelet.

אוֹמְלֶט.

ŏm-LĔT.

381. ——— soft-boiled eggs.

בֵּיצִים רַכּוֹת.

bay-TSEEM ră-KŎT.

382. ——— hard-boiled eggs.

בֵּיצִים קָשׁוֹת.

bay-TSEEM kă-SHŎT.

383. ——— fried eggs.

בֵּיצִים מְטֻגָּנוֹת.

bay-TSEEM m⌣too-gă-NŎT.

384. ——— scrambled eggs.

חֲבִיתָה.

khă-vee-TĂ.

SOUPS AND ENTRÉES

385. I want [some chicken soup].

אֲנִי (רוֹצָה) (רוֹצֶה) [מְרַק עוֹף].

ă-NEE (rŏ-TSĂ F.) (rŏ-TSĔ M.) [m⌣răk ŏf].

386. Vegetable soup.

מְרַק יְרָקוֹת.

m⌣răk y⌣ră-KŎT.

387. Herring.

דָּג מָלוּחַ.

dăg mă-LOO-ăkh.

388. Sardines.

סַרְדִּינִים.

săr-DEE-neem.

389. Fish.

דָּגִים.

dă-GEEM.

390. Liver.

כָּבֵד.

kă-VĔD.

391. Roast chicken.

עוֹף צָלוּי.

ŏf tsă-LOOEY.

392. Duck.

בַּרְוָז.

băr-VĂZ.

393. Lamb.

בְּשַׂר כֶּבֶשׂ.

b⌣săr KĔ-vĕs.

394. Beef.

בְּשַׂר בָּקָר.

b⌣săr bă-KĂR.

395. Roast beef.

בְּשָׂר צָלוּי.

bă-SĂR tsă-LOOEY.

396. Steak.

אֻמְצָה OR סְטֵיק.

oom-TSĂ

397. Veal.

בְּשַׂר עֵגֶל.

b⌣săr Ĕ-gĕl.

VEGETABLES AND SALAD

398. I want some [asparagus].

.[אֲנִי (רוֹצָה) (רוֹצָה) [אַסְפָּרָגוּס]

ă-NEE M. *(rŏ-TSĂ) (rŏ-TSĔ* F.) *[ăs-pă-RĂ-goos]*.

399. Beans.

שְׁעוּעִית.

shֶֿ-EET.

400. Cabbage.

כְּרוּב.

kֶֿroov.

401. Carrots.

גֶּזֶר.

GĔ-zĕr.

402. Cauliflower.

כְּרוּבִית.

kֶֿroo-VEET.

403. Olives.

זֵיתִים.

zay-TEEM.

404. Cucumbers.

מְלָפְפוֹנִים.

mֶֿlăf-fŏ-NEEM.

405. Lettuce.

חַסָּה.

KHĂ-să.

406. Mushrooms.

פִּטְרִיּוֹת.

peet-ree-YŌT.

407. Onions.

בָּצָל.

bă-TSĂL.

408. Peas.

אֲפוּנָה.

ă-foo-NĂ.

409. Peppers.

פִּלְפֵּל יָרוֹק.

peel-PĔL yă-RŎK.

410. Boiled potatoes.

תַּפּוּחֵי־אֲדָמָה מְבֻשָּׁלִים.

tă-poo-KHAY ă-dă-MĂ mֶֿvoo-shă-LEEM.

411. Mashed potatoes.

תַּפּוּחֵי־אֲדָמָה מְעוּכִים.

tă-poo-KHAY ă-dă-MĂ mֶֿoo-KHEEM.

412. Baked potatoes.

תַּפּוּחֵי־אֲדָמָה אֲפוּיִים.

tă-poo-KHAY ă-dă-MĂ ă-foo-YEEM.

413. Rice.

אֹרֶז.

Ŏ-rĕz.

414. Spinach.

תֶּרֶד.

TĔ-rĕd.

415. Tomatoes.

עַגְבָנִיּוֹת.

ăg-vă-nee-YŌT.

FRUITS

416. Do you have [apples]?

הַאִם יֵשׁ (לָכֶם) [תַּפּוּחִים]?

hă-EEM yĕsh (lă-KHEM TO PL.) *[tă-poo-KHEEM]?*

417. Apricots.

מִשְׁמְשִׁים.

meesh-Mֶֿ SHEEM.

418. Bananas.

בַּנָנוֹת.

bă-nă-NŌT.

419. Cherries.

דֻּבְדְּבָנִים.

doov-dֶֿvă-NEEM.

420. Dates.
תְּמָרִים.
t‿mă-REEM.

421. Figs.
תְּאֵנִים.
t‿ĕ-NEEM.

422. A half grapefruit.
חֲצִי אֶשְׁכּוֹלִית.
khă-TSEE ĕsh-kŏ-LEET.

423. Grapes.
עֲנָבִים.
ă-nă-VEEM.

424. Lemons.
לִימוֹנִים.
lee-mŏ-NEEM.

425. An orange.
תַּפּוּז.
tă-POOZ.

426. Pears.
אַגָּסִים.
ă-gă-SEEM.

427. A peach.
אֲפַרְסֵק.
ă-făr-SEK.

428. A piece of melon.
חֲתִיכַת מֶלוֹן.
khă-tee-KHĂT mĕ-LŎN.

429. Raspberries.
פֶּטֶל.
PĔ-tĕl.

430. Strawberries.
תּוּת־שָׂדֶה.
toot să-DĔ.

431. Fruit.
פֵּרוֹת.
pĕ-RŎT.

BEVERAGES

432. A cup of black coffee.
סֵפֶל קָפֶה שָׁחוֹר.
SĔ-fĕl kă-FĔ shă-KHŎR.

433. Coffee with milk.
קָפֶה בְּחָלָב.
kă-FĔ b‿khă-LĂV.

434. A glass of milk.
כּוֹס חָלָב.
kŏs khă-LĂV.

435. Tea with lemon.
תֵּה בְּלִימוֹן.
tĕ b‿lee-MŎN.

436. Lemonade.
לִימוֹנָדָה.
lee-mŏ-NĂ-dă.

437. Soda water with syrup.
גָּזוֹז.
gă-ZŎZ.

DESSERTS

438. I would like to have [a piece of cake].
הָיִיתִי (רוֹצָה) (רוֹצֶה) [חֲתִיכַת עוּגָה].
hă-YEE-tee (rŏ-TSĂ F.) (rŏ-TSĔ M.) [khă-tee-KHĂT oo-GĂ].

439. Apple pie.
עוּגַת תַּפּוּחִים.
oo-GĂT tă-poo-KHEEM.

440. Cookies.
עוּגִיּוֹת.
oo-gee-YŎT.

30

441. Chocolate ice cream.
גְּלִידַת שׁוֹקוֹלָד.
g‿lee-DĂT SHŎ-kŏ-lăd.

442. Vanilla ice cream.
גְּלִידַת וָנִיל.
g‿lee-DĂT vă-NEEL.

RESTAURANT CONVERSATION

443. הַאִם אַתֶּם רוֹצִים מַשֶּׁהוּ מִן הַבָּר?
hă-EEM ă-TĔM rŏ-TSEEM MĂ-shĕ-hoo meen hă-BĂR?
Would you like to have something from the bar?

444. כֵּן, כֵּן, כּוֹסִית אַחַת וֶרְמוּת, כּוֹסִית שֶׁרִי, וּבַקְבּוּק יַיִן לָבָן.
kĕn, kĕn, kŏ-SEET ă-KHĂT vĕr-MOOT, kŏ-SEET SHĔ-ree, oo-văk-BOOK YĂ-yeen lă-VĂN.
Yes, one glass vermouth, one sherry, and a bottle of white wine.

445. הַאִם הֱיִיתֶם רוֹצִים לְהַזְמִין אֶת אֲרוּחַת הָעֶרֶב עַכְשָׁו?
hă-EEM hĕ-yee-TĔM rŏ-TSEEM l‿hăz-MEEN ĕt ă-roo-KHĂT hă-Ĕ-rĕv ăkh-SHĂV?
Would you like to order your dinner now?

446. כֵּן. עַל מָה אַתָּה מַמְלִיץ? מַה טּוֹב אֶצְלְכֶם בִּמְיֻחָד?
kĕn. ăl mă ă-TĂ măm-LEETS? mă TŎV ĕts-L‿KHĔM bee-M‿YOO-khăd?
Yes. What do you recommend? What is especially good here?

447. הָאֻמְצָה שֶׁלָּנוּ טוֹבָה מְאֹד. גַּם הַפִילֶה טָעִים מְאֹד.
hă-oom-TSĂ shĕ-LĂ-noo tŏ-VĂ m‿ŏd. găm hă-fee-LĔ tă-EEM m‿ŏd.
Our steak is very good. The filet of sole is also very tasty.

448. תֵּן לָנוּ בְּבַקָּשָׁה מָנָה אַחַת אֻמְצָה עֲשׂוּיָה הֵיטֵב, וּמָנָה שֶׁל כָּבֵד קָצוּץ.
tĕn LĂ-noo b‿vă-kă-SHĂ mă-NĂ ă-KHĂT oom-TSĂ ă-soo-YĂ hay-TĔV, oo-mă-NĂ shĕl kă-VĔD kă-TSOOTS.
Please give us an order of steak, well done, and one order of chopped liver.

449. תּוּכְלוּ לִבְחֹר בִּשְׁנֵי מִינֵי יְרָקוֹת.
too-KH‿LOO lee-VKHŎR bee-SH‿NAY mee-NAY y‿ră-KŎT.
You can choose two vegetables.

450. עֲגְבָנִיּוֹת וְתַפּוּחֵי־אֲדָמָה אֲפוּיִים עִם הָאֻמְצָה; וְאַסְפָּרָגוּס וּבָצָל מְטֻגָּן
עִם הַכָּבֵד.

ag-vă-nee-YOT v⌣tă-poo-KHAY ă-dă-MĂ ă-foo-YEEM eem hă-
oom-TSĂ; v⌣as-pa-RĂ-goos oo⌣vă-TSĂL m⌣too-GĂN eem hă-
kă-VĔD.

Tomatoes and baked potatoes with the steak; asparagus and
fried onions with the liver.

451. מַה הֱיִיתֶם רוֹצִים לְמָנָה רִאשׁוֹנָה, וְאֵיזֶה מָרָק?

mă hĕ-yee-TĔM rŏ-TSEEM l⌣mă-NĂ ree-shŏ-NĂ, v⌣ay-ZĔ mă-
RĂK?

What would you like for your appetizer and soup course?

452. מָנָה אַחַת שֶׁל דָּג כָּבוּשׁ וּמָנָה אַחַת סָלָט פֵּרוֹת.   מְרַק אֲפוּנָה וְלֶחֶם
לִשְׁנֵינוּ.

mă-NĂ ă-KHĂT shĕl dăg kă-VOOSH oo⌣mă-NĂ ă-KHĂT să-
LĂT pĕ-RŌT. m⌣răk ă-foo-NĂ V⌣LĔ-khĕm lee-SH⌣NAY-noo.

One order of marinated herring and one order of fruit cup.
Pea soup and bread for both of us.

453. סָלָט?

să-LĂT?

Salad?

454. סָלָט יְרָקוֹת, בְּלִי הַרְבֵּה רֹטֶב.   סָלָט חַסָּה וְעֲגְבָנִיּוֹת עִם קְצָת שֶׁמֶן
וְחֹמֶץ—בְּלִי שׁוּם, בְּבַקָּשָׁה.

să-LĂT y⌣ră-KŌT, b⌣lee hăr-BĔ RŌ-tĕv. să-LĂT KHĂ-să
v⌣ăg-vă-nee-YŌT eem k⌣tsăt SHĔ-men V⌣KHŌ-mĕts—b⌣lee
shoom, b⌣vă-kă-SHĂ.

One mixed green salad; not too much dressing. A lettuce
and tomato salad with a little oil and vinegar—no garlic,
please.

455. קָפֶה עִם הָאֲרוּחָה?

kă-FĔ eem ha-a-roo-KHĂ?

Coffee with your dinner?

456. לֹא, לֹא, תּוֹדָה.   קָפֶה וּמָנָה אַחֲרוֹנָה נִקַּח אַחַר־כָּךְ.

lŏ, lŏ, tŏ-DĂ. kă-FĔ oo-mă-NĂ ă-khă-rŏ-NĂ nee-KĂKH ă-KHĂR
kăkh.

No, thank you. We'll have coffee and dessert later.

457. תּוֹדָה. לְמָנָה אַחֲרוֹנָה יֵשׁ לָנוּ: גְּלִידַת שׁוֹקוֹלָד, וָנִיל אוֹ תּוּת־שָׂדֶה,
עוּגִיּוֹת, עוּגַת גְּבִינָה וְעוּגַת שְׁמָרִים.

tŏ-DĂ. l⌣mă-NĂ ă-khă-rŏ-NĂ yĕsh LĂ-noo: g⌣lee-DĂT SHŎ-kŏ-lăd, vă-NEEL ŏ toot să-DĔ, oo-gee-YŌT, oo-GĂT g⌣vee-NĂ v⌣oo-GĂT sh⌣mă-REEM.

Thanks. For dessert we have: chocolate, vanilla, or straw-berry ice cream, assorted pastries, cheese cake and plain cake.

458. אֲנַחְנוּ נִקַּח מָנָה אַחַת גְּלִידַת שׁוֹקוֹלָד, עוּגַת פֵּרוֹת, סֵפֶל קָפֶה שָׁחוֹר,
וְתֵה בְּחָלָב. מֶלְצַר, הָבֵא בְּבַקָּשָׁה סַכִּין אַחֶרֶת. זֹאת אֵינֶנָּה
חַדָּה.

ă-NĂKH-noo nee-KĂKH mă-NĂ ă-KHĂT g⌣lee-DĂT SHŎ-kŏ-lăd, oo-GĂT pĕ-RŌT, SĔ-fĕl kă-FĔ shă-KHŎR, v⌣tĕ b⌣khă-LĂV. mĕl-TSĂR, hă-VĔ b⌣vă-kă-SHĂ să-KEEN ă-KHĔ-rĕt. zŏt ay-NĔ-nă khă-DĂ.

We'll take one chocolate ice cream, one fruit cake, a cup of black coffee, tea with milk. Waiter, please bring another knife. This one isn't sharp.

459. אֲנִי מִצְטַעֵר.

ă-nee meets-tă-ĔR.

I'm sorry.

460. הַאִם נוּכַל לְקַבֵּל אֶת הַחֶשְׁבּוֹן מִיָּד, הַשָּׁעָה כְּבָר מְאֻחֶרֶת, וְלֹא נִשְׁאָר
לָנוּ זְמַן רַב עַד הַתְחָלַת הַהַצָּגָה.

hă-EEM noo-KHĂL l⌣kă-BĔL ĕt hă-khĕsh-BŎN mee-YĂD, hă-shă-Ă k⌣văr m⌣oo-KHĔ-rĕt. v⌣lŏ neesh-ĂR LĂ-noo z⌣măn răv ăd hăt-khă-LĂT hă-hă-tsă-GĂ.

May we have our check right away, because it is late. We haven't got much time left before the play starts.

461. כֵּן, אֲדוֹנִי.

kĕn, ă-dŏ-NEE.

Yes, sir.

CHURCH AND SYNAGOGUE

462. Is there [an English-speaking rabbi]?
הַאִם יֵשׁ כָּאן [רַב דּוֹבֵר אַנְגְּלִית]?
hă-EEM yĕsh kăn [răv dŏ-VĔR ăng-LEET]?

463. ——— a priest.	**464.** ——— a minister.
כֹּמֶר קָתוֹלִי.	כֹּמֶר פְּרוֹטֶסְטַנְטִי.
KŎ-mĕr kă-tŏ-LEE.	*KŎ-mĕr prŏ-tĕs-TĂN-tee.*

465. ——— a synagogue.
בֵּית־כְּנֶסֶת.
bayt KNĔ-sĕt.

466. ——— a Catholic church.
כְּנֵסִיָּה קַתּוֹלִית.
k⌣nĕ-see-YÄ kă-tŏ-LEET.

467. ——— a Protestant church.
כְּנֵסִיָּה פְּרוֹטֶסְטַנְטִית.
k⌣nĕ-see-YÄ prŏ-tĕs-TÄN-teet.

468. ——— a mosque.
מִסְגָּד.
mees-GÄD.

469. When is the service?
מָתַי הַתְּפִלָּה?
mă-TÍ hă-t⌣fee-LÄ?

SIGHTSEEING

470. We want [a licensed guide] who speaks English.
אֲנַחְנוּ רוֹצִים [מוֹרֵה־דֶּרֶךְ מוּסְמָךְ] הַמְדַבֵּר אַנְגְּלִית.
ă-NÄKH-noo rŏ-TSEEM [mŏ-RĔ DĔ-rĕkh moos-MÄKH] hă-
m⌣dă-BĔR ăng-LEET.

471. How much does this cost [per hour]?
כַּמָּה זֶה עוֹלֶה [לְשָׁעָה]?
kă-MÄ zĕ ŏ-LĔ [l⌣shă-Ä]?

472. ——— per day.
לְיוֹם.
l⌣yŏm.

473. I am interested [in architecture].
אֲנִי (מִתְעַנֵּין) (מִתְעַנֵּינֶת) [בְּאַדְרִיכָלוּת].
ă-NEE (meet-ăn-YĔN м.) (meet-ăn-YĔ-nĕt ꜰ.) [b⌣ăd-ree-khă-
LOOT].

474. ——— in painting.
בְּצִיּוּר.
b⌣tsee-YOOR.

475. ——— in sculpture.
בְּפִסּוּל.
b⌣fee-SOOL.

476. Show us [the most important places].
הַרְאֵה לָנוּ אֶת [הַמְּקוֹמוֹת הַחֲשׁוּבִים בְּיוֹתֵר].
(hăr-Ĕ ᴛᴏ м.) (hăr-EE ᴛᴏ ꜰ.) LÄ-noo ĕt [ha-m⌣kŏ-MŎT hă-khă-
shoo-VEEM b⌣yŏ-TĔR].

477. ——— the Great Synagogue.
בֵּית־הַכְּנֶסֶת הַגָּדוֹל.
bayt hă-K⌣NĔ-sĕt hă-gă-DŎL.

478. ——— the Crusaders' castle.
הַמַּצְלֵבָה.
hă-măts-lĕ-VÄ.

479. ——— the Knesset.

הַכְּנֶסֶת.

hă-K⏝NĔ-sĕt.

480. We want to visit [a collective farm.]

אֲנַחְנוּ רוֹצִים לְבַקֵּר [בְּקִבּוּץ].

ă-NĂKH-noo rŏ-TSEEM l⏝vă-KĔR [b⏝kee-BOOTS].

481. ——— a cooperative farm.

בְּמוֹשָׁב.

b⏝mŏ-SHĂV.

482. ——— a nursery school.

בְּבֵית תִּינוֹקוֹת.

b⏝vayt tee-nŏ-KŌT.

483. ——— the Habima theater.

בְּתֵאַטְרוֹן «הַבִּימָה».

b⏝tĕ-ăt-RŌN "hă-bee-MĂ".

484. ——— the potash works.

בְּמִפְעַל הָאַשְׁלָג.

b⏝meef-ĂL hă-ăsh-LĂG.

485. When does it [open]?

מָתַי זֶה [נִפְתָּח]?

mă-TĪ zĕ [neef-TĂKH]?

486. ——— close.

נִסְגָּר.

nees-GĂR.

487. Where is [the entrance]?

אֵיפֹה [הַכְּנִיסָה]?

ay-FŌ [hă-k⏝nee-SĂ]?

488. ——— the exit.

הַיְצִיאָה.

hă-y⏝tsee-Ă.

AMUSEMENTS

489. I should like to go [to a concert].

הָיִיתִי (רוֹצֶה) (רוֹצָה) לָלֶכֶת [לְקוֹנְצֶרְט].

hă-YEE-tee (rŏ-TSĔ M.) (rŏ-TSĂ F.) lă-LĔ-khĕt [l⏝kön-TSĔRT].

490. ——— to the ballet.

לַבָּלֶט.

lă-bă-LĔT.

491. ——— to the circus.

לַקִּרְקָס.

lă-keer-KĂS.

492. ——— to the movies.

לַקּוֹלְנוֹעַ.

lă-köl-NŌ-ă.

493. ——— to a night club.

לְמוֹעֲדוֹן לַיְלָה.

l⏝mŏ-ă-DŌN LĪ-lă.

494. ——— to the opera.

לָאוֹפֵּרָה.

lă-Ō-pĕ-ră.

495. ——— to the theater.

לַתֵּאַטְרוֹן.

lă-tĕ-ăt-RŌN.

496. ——— to a matinee.

לְהַצָּגָה יוֹמִית.

l⏝hă-tsă-GĂ yŏ-MEET.

497. ——— to the box office.

לַקֻּפָּה.

lă-koo-PĂ.

498. What is playing [this evening]?

מַה מַצִּינִים [הָעֶרֶב]?

mă mă-tsee-GEEM [hă-Ĕ-rĕv]?

499. How much is [the admission charge]?

כַּמָּה עוֹלֶה [כַּרְטִיס הַכְּנִיסָה]?

kă-MĂ ŏ-LĔ [kăr-TEES hă-knee-SĂ]?

500. When will [the evening performance] start?

מָתַי מַתְחִילָה [הַצָּגַת הָעֶרֶב]?

mă-TĬ măt-khee-LĂ [hă-tsă-GĂT hă-Ĕ-rĕv]?

501. When will [the intermission] begin?

מָתַי מַתְחִילָה [הַהַפְסָקָה]?

mă-TĬ măt-khee-LĂ [hă-hăf-să-KĂ]?

502. Do you (PL.) have orchestra seats for tonight?

הַאִם יֵשׁ לָכֶם מְקוֹמוֹת בָּאוּלָם לְהָעֶרֶב?

hă-EEM yĕsh lă-KHĔM mꞈkŏ-MŌT bă-oo-LAM lꞈhă-Ĕ-rĕv?

503. Have you [a balcony seat]?

הַאִם יֵשׁ לָכֶם [מָקוֹם בַּיָּצִיעַ]?

hă-EEM yĕsh lă-KHĔM [mă-KŎM bă-yă-TSEE-ă]?

504. Have you [a box seat]?

הַאִם יֵשׁ לָכֶם [מָקוֹם בְּתָא]?

hă-EEM yĕsh lă-KHĔM [mă-KŎM bꞈtă]?

505. Is it possible to see and hear well from there?

הַאִם אֶפְשָׁר לִרְאוֹת וְלִשְׁמֹעַ מִשָּׁם הֵיטֵב?

hă-EEM ĕf-SHAR leer-ŌT vꞈleesh-MŌ-ă mee-SHĂM hay-TĔV?

506. Where will we be able to dance?

אֵיפֹה יֵשׁ כָּאן מָקוֹם לִרְקֹד?

ay-FŌ yĕsh kăn mă-KŎM leer-KŎD?

507. May I have this dance?

הַאִם אוּכַל לְהַזְמִין אוֹתָךְ לָרִקּוּד הַזֶּה?

hă-EEM oo-KHĂL lꞈhăz-MEEN ŏ-TĂKH lă-ree-KOOD hă-ZĔ?

SPORTS

508. Let's go [to the beach].

הָבָה נֵלֵךְ [לִשְׂפַת הַיָּם].

HĂ-vă nĕ-LĔKH [lee-SꞈFĂT hă-YĂM].

509. ——— to the basketball game.

לְמִשְׂחַק הַכַּדּוּרְסַל.

└mees-KHĂK hă-kă-door-SĂL.

510. ——— to the soccer game.

לְמִשְׂחַק הַכַּדּוּרֶגֶל.

└mees-KHĂK hă-kă-doo-RĔ-gĕl.

511. ——— to the swimming pool.

לִבְרֵכַת הַשְּׂחִיָּה.

lee-v└rĕ-KHĂT hă-s└khee-YĂ.

512. Can we go [fishing]?

הַאִם נוּכַל לָלֶכֶת [לָדוּג]?

hă-EEM noo-KHĂL lă-LĔ-khĕt [lă-DOOG]?

513. ——— horseback riding.

לִרְכַּב עַל סוּסִים.

leer-KĂV ăl soo-SEEM.

514. ——— swimming.

לִשְׂחוֹת.

lees-KHŎT.

BANK AND MONEY

515. Where can I change [foreign money]?

אֵיפֹה אוּכַל לְהַחֲלִיף [מַטְבֵּעַ זַר]?

ay-FŎ oo-KHĂL └hă-khă-LEEF [măt-BĔ-ă zăr]?

516. Where is [the bank] located?

אֵיפֹה נִמְצָא [הַבַּנְק]?

ay-FŎ neem-TSĂ [hă-BĂNK]?

517. Could you cash [a personal check] for me?

הַאִם (תּוּכַל TO M.) (תּוּכְלִי TO F.) לִפְרֹעַ לִי [הַמְחָאָה אִישִׁית]?

hă-EEM (too-KHĂL TO M.) (too-KH└LEE TO F.) leef-RŎ-ă lee [hăm-khă-Ă ee-SHEET]?

518. ——— a traveler's check.

הַמְחָאַת נוֹסֵעַ.

hăm-khă-ĂT nŏ-SĔ-ă.

519. What is [the exchange rate] on the dollar?

מַהוּ [שַׁעַר הַחֲלִיפִין] שֶׁל הַדּוֹלָר?

MĂ-hoo [SHĂ-ăr hă-khă-lee-FEEN] shĕl hă-DŎ-lăr?

520. Could I change [fifty dollars] into Israel pounds?

הַאָם אוּכַל לְהַחֲלִיף [חֲמִשִּׁים דּוֹלָר] בְּלִירוֹת יִשְׂרְאֵלִיוֹת?

hă-EEM oo-KHĂL Lⱼhă-khă-LEEF [khă-mee-SHEEM DŎ-lär] bⱼlee-RŌT yees-rⱼĕ-lee-YŌT?

521. May I have [some large bills]?

הַאָם אוּכַל לְקַבֵּל [כַּמָּה שְׁטָרוֹת בְּסְכוּמִים גְּדוֹלִים]?

hă-EEM oo-KHĂL Lⱼkă-BĚL [kă-MĂ shⱼtă-RŌT bee-sⱼkhoo-MEEM gⱼdö-LEEM]?

522. —— small bills.

כַּמָּה שְׁטָרוֹת בְּסְכוּמִים קְטַנִּים.

kă-MĂ shⱼtă-RŌT bee-sⱼkhoo-MEEM kⱼtă-NEEM.

523. —— change.

קְצָת כֶּסֶף קָטָן.

kⱼtsăt KĚ-sĕf kă-TĂN.

POST OFFICE CONVERSATION

524. אֲנִי רוֹצֶה לִשְׁלֹחַ אֶת הַמִּכְתָּב הַזֶּה לְאַרְצוֹת־הַבְּרִית.   כַּמָּה בּוּלִים דְּרוּשִׁים לִי?

ă-NEE rŏ-TSĚ leesh-LŌ-ăkh ĕt hă-meekh-TĂV hă-ZĚ Lⱼär-TSŌT hă-BⱼREET. kă-MĂ boo-LEEM dⱼroo-SHEEM lee?

I'd like to send this letter to the United States. How much postage do I need?

525. בְּדֹאַר רָגִיל, אוֹ בְּדֹאַר אֲוִיר?

BⱼDŎ-är ră-GEEL, ŏ BⱼDŎ-är ă-VEER?

By regular mail, or by air mail?

526. בְּדֹאַר אֲוִיר, בְּבַקָּשָׁה.

BⱼDŎ-är ă-VEER, bⱼvă-kă-SHĂ.

By air mail; please.

527. הַמְחִיר הוּא חֲמִשִּׁים אֲגוֹרוֹת בְּעַד כָּל עֲשָׂרָה גְרָם.   אִגֶּרֶת אֲוִיר עוֹלָה שְׁלוֹשִׁים וְחָמֵשׁ אֲגוֹרוֹת.

hă-MⱼKHEER hoo khă-mee-SHEEM ă-gŏ-RŌT bⱼăd köl ă-să-RĂ gⱼrăm. ee-GĚ-rĕt ă-VEER ŏ-LĂ shⱼlö-SHEEM vⱼkhă-MĚSH ă-gŏ-RŌT.

The fee is 50 agorot for (every) 10 grams. An air letter costs 35 agorot.

528. תְּנִי לִי בְּבַקָּשָׁה חֲמִשָּׁה בּוּלִים שֶׁל חֲמִשִּׁים אֲגוֹרוֹת וְעֶשֶׂר אִגְּרוֹת אֲוִיר.

*t∪nee lee b∪vă-kă-SHĂ khă-mee-SHĂ boo-LEEM shĕl khă-mee-
SHEEM ă-gŏ-RŎT V∪Ė-sĕr ee-G∪RŎT ă-VEER.*

Please give me five 50 agorot stamps and 10 air letters.

529. בְּבַקָּשָׁה. אַתָּה חַיָּב לִי שֵׁשׁ לִירוֹת בְּעַד הַבּוּלִים וְהָאִגְּרוֹת.

*b∪vă-kă-SHĂ. ă-TĂ khă-YĂV lee shĕsh lee-RŎT b∪ăd hă-boo-
LEEM v∪hă-ee-G∪RŎT.*

Here they are. You owe me IL. 6 for the stamps and the air
letters.

530. תּוֹדָה. אֶל מִי עָלַי לִפְנוֹת כְּדֵי לִשְׁלֹחַ מַשֶּׁהוּ בִּדְאַר חֲבִילוֹת?

*tŏ-DĂ. ĕl MEE ă-LI leef-NŎT k∪day leesh-LŎ-ăkh MĂ-shĕ-hoo
B∪DŎ-ăr khă-vee-LŎT.*

Thank you. Where do I go to send a package by parcel post?

531. אֲנִי אוּכַל לְסַדֵּר לְךָ אֶת זֶה. מַה יֵשׁ בַּחֲבִילָה?

*ă-NEE oo-KHĂL ∪să-DĔR ∪khă ĕt zĕ. mă yĕsh bă-khă-vee-
LĂ?*

I can take care of it for you. What is in the package?

532. רַק סְפָרִים.

răk s∪fă-REEM.

Only books.

533. סְפָרִים חֲדָשִׁים?

s∪fă-REEM khă-dă-SHEEM?

New books?

534. לֹא, כֻּלָּם יְשָׁנִים. אֵין שׁוּם דָּבָר שָׁבִיר בִּפְנִים. הַאִם אוּכַל לִשְׁלֹחַ
אוֹתָם בִּדְאַר רָשׁוּם?

*lŏ, koo-LĂM y∪shă-NEEM. ayn shoom dă-VĂR shă-VEER bee-
F∪NEEM. hă-EEM oo-KHĂL leesh-LŎ-ăkh ŏ-TĂM B∪DŎ-
ăr ră-SHOOM?*

No, they are all old. Nothing fragile inside. Could I send
them by registered mail?

535. כֵּן, כַּמּוּבָן.

kĕn, kă-moo-VĂN.

Yes, of course.

536. הָיִיתִי רוֹצֶה לְבַטֵּחַ אֶת הַחֲבִילָה בַּחֲמִשִּׁים לִירוֹת.

*hă-YEE-tee ro-TSĔ ∪vă-TĔ-ăkh ĕt hă-khă-vee-LĂ bă-khă-mee-
SHEEM lee-RŎT.*

I should like to insure this for IL. 50.

537. מַלֵּא בְּבַקָּשָׁה אֶת הַטֹּפֶס הַזֶּה. הַמִּשְׁקָל הוּא קִילוֹ וָחֵצִי. הַמְּחִיר הַכּוֹלֵל הוּא שָׁלוֹשׁ לִירוֹת: שְׁתֵּי לִירוֹת עֲבוּר הַבּוּלִים וְלִירָה אַחַת עֲבוּר הָרִשּׁוּם.

mă-LĚ b⌣vă-kă-SHĂ ĕt hă-TŎ-fĕs hă-ZĚ. hă-meesh-KĂL hoo
KEE-lŏ vă-KHĚ-tsee. hă-M⌣KHEER hă-kŏ-LĚL hoo shă-
LŎSH lee-RŌT: sh⌣tay lee-RŌT ă-VOOR hă-boo-LEEM
V⌣LEE-ră ă-KHĂT ă-VOOR hă-ree-SHOOM.

Please fill out this form. The weight is 1½ kilograms (3 pounds).
The total charge is IL. 3. IL. 2 for postage and IL. 1 for
registration.

538. הַאִם תּוּכְלִי לָתֵת לִי אֶת הַקַּבָּלָה?

hă-EEM too-KH⌣LEE lă-TĚT lee ĕt hă-kă-bă-LĂ?

Could you give me the receipt?

539. כַּמּוּבָן. חֲתֹם בְּבַקָּשָׁה אֶת שִׁמְךָ מֵעַל לַקַּו הַזֶּה. עַל הַקִּיר תְּלוּיָה תֵּבַת דֹּאַר. עוֹד מַשֶּׁהוּ?

kă-moo-VĂN. khă-TŎM b⌣vă-kă-SHĂ ĕt shee-M⌣KHĂ mĕ-ĂL
lă-KĂV hă-ZĚ. ăl hă-KEER t⌣loo-YĂ tay-VĂT DŌ-ăr. ŏd
MĂ-she-hoo?

Yes. Please sign your name above this line. There's a mail-
box against the wall. Anything else?

540. לֹא, זֶה הַכֹּל, תּוֹדָה רַבָּה.

lŏ, zĕ hă-KŎL, tŏ-DĂ ră-BĂ.

Nothing, thanks very much.

SHOPPING

541. I want to go shopping.
אֲנִי (רוֹצָה) (רוֹצֶה) לַעֲרֹךְ קְנִיּוֹת.
ă-NEE (rŏ-TSĂ F.) (rŏ-TSĚ M.) lă-ă-RŌKH k⌣nee-YŌT.

542. What can I do for you?
מָה אוּכַל לַעֲשׂוֹת (בִּשְׁבִילֵךְ) (בִּשְׁבִילְךָ)?
mă oo-KHĂL lă-ă-SŌT (bee-sh⌣vee-LĚKH TO F.) (bee-sh⌣vee-
L⌣KHĂ TO M.)?

543. I do not like this one.
זֶה לֹא מוֹצֵא חֵן בְּעֵינַי.
zĕ lŏ mŏ-TSĚ khĕn b⌣ay-NĪ.

544. How much is it?
כַּמָּה זֶה עוֹלֶה?
kă-MĂ zĕ ŏ-LĚ?

545. The price is [1 pound 30].
הַמְּחִיר הוּא [לִירָה וּשְׁלוֹשִׁים אֲגוֹרוֹת].
hă-M⌣KHEER hoo LEE-ră [oo-sh⌣lŏ-SHEEM ă-gŏ-RŌT].

546. Is this your (PL.) lowest price?

הַאִם זֶה הַמְּחִיר הַנָּמוּךְ בְּיוֹתֵר אֶצְלְכֶם?

*hă-EEM zĕ hă-M⌣KHEER hă-nă-MOOKH b⌣yŏ-TĔR ĕts-
L⌣KHĔM?*

547. I prefer something [better].

אֲנִי (מַעֲדִיפָה) (מַעֲדִיף) מַשֶּׁהוּ [יוֹתֵר טוֹב].

*ă-NEE (mă-ă-dee-FĂ F.) (mă-ă-DEEF M.) MĂ-shĕ-hoo [yŏ-TĔR
tŏv].*

548. ——— cheaper.

יוֹתֵר זוֹל.

yŏ-TĔR zŏl.

549. ——— larger.

יוֹתֵר גָּדוֹל.

yŏ-TĔR gă-DŎL.

550. ——— smaller.

יוֹתֵר קָטָן.

yŏ-TĔR kă-TĂN.

551. ——— stronger.

יוֹתֵר חָזָק.

yŏ-TĔR khă-ZĂK.

552. May I try this on?

הַאִם אוּכַל לִמְדֹּד אֶת זֶה?

hă-EEM oo-KHĂL leem-DŎD ĕt zĕ?

553. Can I order the same thing [in size 32]?

הַאִם אוּכַל לְהַזְמִין אוֹתוֹ הַדָּבָר [בְּמִסְפָּר שְׁלֹשִׁים וּשְׁתַּיִם]?

*hă-EEM oo-KHĂL l⌣hăz-MEEN ŏ-TŎ hă-dă-VĂR [b⌣mees-
PĂR sh⌣lŏ-SHEEM oo-SH⌣TĂ-yeem]?*

554. Please take [the measurements].

(קְחִי) (קַח) אֶת [הַמִּדּוֹת] בְּבַקָּשָׁה.

(k⌣khee TO F.) (kăkh TO M.) ĕt [hă-mee-DŎT] b⌣vă-kă-SHĂ.

555. ——— the length.

הָאֹרֶךְ.

hă-Ŏ-rĕkh.

556. ——— the width.

הָרֹחַב.

hă-RŎ-khăv.

557. When will it be ready?

מָתַי זֶה יִהְיֶה מוּכָן?

mă-TĪ zĕ yee-H⌣YĔ moo-KHĂN?

558. Can you ship it to New York?

הַאִם (תּוּכְלִי) (תּוּכַל) לִשְׁלֹחַ אֶת זֶה לְנִיוּ־יוֹרְק?

*hă-EEM (too-KH⌣LEE TO F.) (too-KHĂL TO M.) leesh-LŎ-ăkh ĕt
zĕ lee-"New York"?*

559. Do I have to pay [the salesgirl]?

הַאִם עָלַי לְשַׁלֵּם [לַזַּבָּנִית]?

hă-EEM ă-LĪ l⌣shă-LĔM [lă-ză-bă-NEET]?

560. ———— the salesman.

לַזַּבָּן.

lă-ză-BĂN.

561. ———— the cashier.

לַקֻפָּאי.*

lă-koo-pă-EE.

562. Please give me an itemized bill.

(תְּנִי) (תֵּן) לִי בְּבַקָּשָׁה חֶשְׁבּוֹן מְפֹרָט.

(*t̬nee* TO F.) (*tĕn* TO M.) *lee b̬vă-kă-SHĂ khĕsh-BŎN m̬fŏ-RĂT.*

563. Wrap it carefully; it's for export.

(אִרְזִי) (אֱרֹז) אֶת זֶה בִּזְהִירוּת; זֶה לְיִצּוּא.

(*eer-ZEE* TO F.) (*ĕ-RŎZ* TO M.) *ĕt zĕ bee-z̬hee-ROOT; zĕ l̬yee-TSOO.*

CLOTHING

564. I want to buy [a bathing cap].

אֲנִי (רוֹצָה) (רוֹצֶה) לִקְנֹת [כּוֹבַע־יָם].

ă-NEE (rŏ-TSĂ F.) (*rŏ-TSĚ* M.) *leek-NŎT [kŏ-VĂ yăm].*

565. A bathing suit.

בֶּגֶד־יָם.

BĚ-gĕd yăm.

566. A brassiere.

חֲזִיָּה.

khă-zee-YĂ.

567. A coat.

מְעִיל עֶלְיוֹן.

m̬eel ĕl-YŎN.

568. A dress.

שִׂמְלָה.

seem-LĂ.

569. A pair of gloves.

זוּג כְּפָפוֹת.

zoog k̬fa-FŎT.

570. A handbag.

אַרְנָק.

ăr-NĂK.

571. A hat.

כּוֹבַע.

kŏ-VĂ.

572. A jacket.

מְעִיל קָצָר.

m̬eel kă-TSĂR.

573. A nightgown.

כֻּתֹּנֶת לַיְלָה.

K̬TŎ-nĕt LI-lă.

574. A raincoat.

מְעִיל־גֶּשֶׁם.

m̬eel GĚ-shĕm.

575. A pair of boots.

זוּג מַגָּפַיִם.

zoog mă-gă-FĂ-yeem.

576. A pair of shoes.

זוּג נַעֲלַיִם.

zoog nă-ă-LĂ-yeem.

577. Shoelaces.

שְׂרוֹכֵי נַעֲלָיִם.

s̬rŏ-KHAY nă-ă-LĂ-yeem.

578. A skirt.

חֲצָאִית.

khă-tsă-EET.

579. A pair of slippers.

זוּג נַעֲלֵי־בַּיִת.

zoog nă-ă-LAY BĂ-yeet.

580. A pair of socks.

זוּג גַּרְבַּיִם קְצָרוֹת.

zoog găr-BĂ-yeem k̬tsă-RŎT.

*Should be לַקֻפַּאי (*lă-koo-PI*).

581. A pair of nylon stockings.

זוּג גַּרְבֵּי נַיְלוֹן.

zoog găr-BAY NĬ-lŏn.

582. A suit.

חֲלִיפָה.

khă-lee-FĂ.

583. A woolen sweater.

אֲפוּדָה.

ă-foo-DĂ.

584. Neckties.

עֲנִיבוֹת.

ă-nee-VŎT.

585. A shirt.

חֻלְצָה.*

khool-TSĂ.

586. A pair of shorts.

זוּג מִכְנָסַיִם קְצָרוֹת.

zoog meekh-nă-SĂ-yeem k⌣tsă-RŎT.

587. A pair of trousers.

זוּג מִכְנָסַיִם.

zoog meekh-nă-SĂ-yeem.

588. A pair of shorts (underwear).

זוּג תַּחְתּוֹנִים.

zoog tăkh-tŏ-NEEM.

589. Undershirts.

גּוּפִיּוֹת.

goo-fee-YŎT.

MISCELLANEOUS ARTICLES

590. Do you (PL.) have [any ashtrays]?

הַאִם יֵשׁ לָכֶם [מַאֲפֵרוֹת]?

hă-EEM yĕsh lă-KHĔM [mă-ă-fĕ-RŎT]?

591. A box of candy.

קֻפְסַת מַמְתַּקִּים.

koof-SĂT măm-tă-KEEM.

592. A deck of playing cards.

חֲבִילַת קְלָפִים.

khă-vee-LĂT k⌣lă-FEEM.

593. China.

כְּלֵי חַרְסִינָה.

k⌣lay khăr-see-NĂ.

594. A silver compact.

מַעֲרֶכֶת כְּלֵי כֶּסֶף.

mă-ă-RĔ-khĕt k⌣lay KĔ-sĕf.

595. Dolls.

בֻּבּוֹת.

boo-BŎT.

596. Earrings.

עֲגִילִים.

a-gee-LEEM.

597. Musical instruments.

כְּלֵי־נְגִינָה.

k⌣lay n⌣gee-NĂ.

598. Perfume.

מֵי בֹּשֶׂם.

may BŎ-sĕm.

599. Pictures.

תְּמוּנוֹת.

t⌣moo-NŎT.

600. Pottery.

כְּלֵי־חֶרֶס.

k⌣lay KHĔ-rĕs.

---

* LIT. blouse. A man's shirt is כֻּתֹּנֶת (K⌣ TŎ-nĕt).

601. Records.

תַּקְלִיטִים.

tăk-lee-TEEM.

602. Silverware.

כְּלֵי־כֶסֶף.

k͜lay KĔ-sĕf.

603. Souvenirs.

מַזְכָּרוֹת.

măz-kă-RŌT.

604. Toys.

צַעֲצוּעִים.

tsă-ă-tsoo-EEM.

605. A silk umbrella.

מִטְרִיַּת מֶשִׁי.

meet-ree-YĂT MĔ-shee.

606. A wristwatch.

שְׁעוֹן־יָד.

sh͜ŏn yăd.

COLORS

607. I want [a lighter shade].

אֲנִי (רוֹצָה) (רוֹצֶה) [גַּן יוֹתֵר בָּהִיר].

ă-NEE (rŏ-TSĂ F.) (rŏ-TSĔ M.) [gă-VĂN yŏ-TĔR bă-HEER].

608. ———— a darker shade.

גַּן יוֹתֵר כֵּהֶה.

gă-VĂN yŏ-TĔR kĕ-HĔ.

609. Black.

שָׁחוֹר.

shă-KHŎR.

610. Blue.

כָּחֹל.

kă-KHŎL.

611. Brown.

חוּם.

khoom.

612. Gray.

אָפֹר.

ă-FŎR.

613. Green.

יָרֹק.

yă-RŎK.

614. Orange.

כָּתֹם.

kă-TŎM.

615. Pink.

וָרֹד.

vă-RŎD.

616. Purple.

אַרְגָּמָן.

ăr-gă-MĂN.

617. Red.

אָדֹם.

ă-DŎM.

618. White.

לָבָן.

lă-VĂN.

619. Yellow.

צָהֹב.

tsă-HŎV.

STORES

620. Where can I find [a bakery] around here?

אֵיפֹה אוּכַל לִמְצֹא כָּאן [מַאֲפִיָה]?

ay-FŎ oo-KHĂL leem-TSŎ kăn [mă-ă-fee-YĂ]?

621. ———— a candy store.

חֲנוּת מַמְתַּקִים.

khă-NOOT măm-tă-KEEM.

622. ———— a tobacco store.

חֲנוּת לְטַבַּק.

khă-NOOT l͜tă-BĂK.

623. ———— a clothing store.
חֲנוּת בְּגָדִים.
khă-NOOT bˍgă-DEEM.

624. ———— a department store.
חֲנוּת כָּל־בּוֹ.
khă-NOOT kol-BÓ.

625. ———— a drugstore.
בֵּית־מִרְקַחַת.
bayt meer-KÄ-khăt.

626. ———— a grocery.
חֲנוּת מַכֹּלֶת.
khă-NOOT mă-KÖ-lĕt.

627. ———— a vegetable shop.
חֲנוּת יְרָקוֹת.
khă-NOOT yˍră-KÖT.

628. ———— a hardware store.
חֲנוּת לִכְלֵי בַּיִת וּמִטְבָּח.
khă-NOOT lee-KHˍLAY BÄ-yeet oo-meet-BÄKH.

629. ———— a jewelry store.
חֲנוּת תַּכְשִׁיטִים.
khă-NOOT tăkh-shee-TEEM.

630. ———— a market.
שׁוּק.
shook.

631. ———— a meat shop.
אִטְלִיז.
eet-LEEZ.

632. ———— a shoe store.
חֲנוּת נַעֲלַיִם.
khă-NOOT nă-ă-LÄ-yeem.

633. ———— a tailor.
חַיָּט.
khă-YÄT.

634. ———— a watchmaker.
שָׁעָן.
shă-ÄN.

BOOKSTORE AND STATIONER'S

635. Where can I find [a bookstore] around here?
אֵיפֹה אוּכַל לִמְצֹא כָּאן [חֲנוּת סְפָרִים]?
ay-FÖ oo-KHÄL leem-TSÖ kăn [khă-NOOT sˍfă-REEM]?

636. ———— a stationer's.
חֲנוּת לְמַכְשִׁירֵי כְּתִיבָה.
khă-NOOT lˍmăkh-shee-RAY kˍtee-VÄ.

637. ———— a news dealer.
מוֹכֵר עִתּוֹנִים.
mŏ-KHER ee-tŏ-NEEM.

638. I want to buy [a book].
אֲנִי (רוֹצֶה) (רוֹצָה) לִקְנֹת [סֵפֶר].
ă-NEE (rŏ-TSĚ m.) (rŏ-TSÄ f.) leek-NÖT [SĚ-fĕr].

639. ——— a tourist guidebook.

מַדְרִיךְ לְתַיָרִים.

mǎd-REEKH l⏜tǎ-yǎ-REEM.

640. ——— a dictionary.

מִלוֹן.

mee-LÔN.

641. ——— a magazine.

עִתּוֹן מְצֻיָר.

ee-TÔN m⏜tsoo-YÂR.

642. ——— a map of Israel.

מַפָּה שֶׁל יִשְׂרָאֵל.

mǎ-PÂ shĕl yees-rǎ-ĔL.

643. ——— a newspaper.

עִתּוֹן.

ee-TÔN.

644. ——— envelopes.

מַעֲטָפוֹת.

mǎ-ǎ-tǎ-FÔT.

645. ——— writing paper.

נְיָר כְּתִיבָה.

n⏜yǎr k⏜tee-VÂ.

646. ——— a fountain pen.

עֵט נוֹבֵעַ.

ĕt nŏ-VĔ-ǎ.

647. ——— a pencil.

עִפָּרוֹן.

ee-pǎ-RÔN.

648. ——— postcards.

גְּלוּיוֹת.

g⏜loo-YÔT.

CIGAR STORE

649. Where is the nearest [cigar store]?

אֵיפֹה [חֲנוּת הַטַּבַּק] הַקְרוֹבָה בְּיוֹתֵר?

ay-FÔ [khǎ-NOOT hǎ-tǎ-BÂK] hǎ-k⏜rŏ-VÂ b⏜yŏ-TĔR?

650. What kinds of cigars do you (PL.) have?

אֵילוּ מִינֵי סִיגָרוֹת יֵשׁ לָכֶם?

AY-loo mee-NAY see-GÂ-röt yĕsh lǎ-KHĔM ?

651. I want to buy [a pack of American cigarettes].

אֲנִי (רוֹצֶה) (רוֹצָה) לִקְנֹת [חֲפִיסַת סִיגָרִיוֹת אֲמֶרִיקָנִיוֹת].

ǎ-NEE (rŏ-TSĔ M.) (rŏ-TSÂ F.) leek-NÔT [khǎ-fee-SAT see-gǎ-ree-YÔT ǎ-mĕ-ree-kǎ-nee-YÔT].

652. ——— a lighter.

מַצִּית.

mǎ-TSEET.

653. ——— pipe tobacco.

טַבַּק לְמִקְטֶרֶת.

tǎ-BÂK l⏜meek-TĔ-rĕt.

654. May I have [a match]?

הַאִם אֶפְשָׁר לְבַקֵּשׁ [גַּפְרוּר]?

hǎ-EEM ĕf-SHÂR l⏜vǎ-KĔSH [gǎf-ROOR]?

CAMERA SHOP

655. I want a roll of film for this camera.

אֲנִי (רוֹצֶה) (רוֹצָה) סֶרֶט בִּשְׁבִיל הַמַּצְלֵמָה הַזֹּאת.

ă-NEE (rŏ-TSĔ M.) (rŏ-TSĂ F.) SĔ-rĕt beesh-VEEL hă-măts-lĕ-MĂ hă-ZŎT.

656. What is the charge for developing [the film]?

כַּמָּה עוֹלֶה פִּתּוּחַ [הַסֶּרֶט]?

kă-MĂ ŏ-LĔ pee-TOO-ăkh [hă-SĔ-rĕt]?

657. When will it be ready?

מָתַי זֶה יִהְיֶה מוּכָן?

mă-TI zĕ yee-H⌣YĔ moo-KHĂN?

658. May I take a snapshot of you?

הַאִם אֶפְשָׁר לְצַלֵּם (אוֹתְךָ) (אוֹתָךְ)?

hă-EEM ĕf-SHĂR ⌣tsă-LĔM (ŏ-T⌣KHĂ TO M.) (ŏ-TĂKH TO F.)?

DRUGSTORE

659. Do you know a pharmacy where they understand English?

הַאִם (אַתָּה מַכִּיר) (אַתְּ מַכִּירָה) בֵּית־מִרְקַחַת שֶׁבּוֹ שׁוֹמְעִים אַנְגְלִית?

hă-EEM (ă-TĂ mă-KEER TO M.) (ăt mă-kee-RĂ TO F.) bayt meer-KĂ-khăt shĕ-BŎ shŏ-M⌣EEM ăng-LEET?

660. May I speak to [the pharmacist]?

הַאִם אוּכַל לְדַבֵּר עִם [הָרוֹקֵחַ]?

hă-EEM oo-KHĂL ⌣dă-BĔR eem [hă-rŏ-KĔ-ăkh M.]?

661. Can you (PL.) prepare this [prescription] immediately?

הַאִם תּוּכְלוּ לְהָכִין אֶת [הַתְּרוּפָה] הַזֹּאת מִיָּד?

hă-EEM too-KH⌣LOO (PL.) ⌣hă-KHEEN ĕt [hă-t⌣roo-FĂ] hă-ZŎT mee-YĂD?

662. I'll wait for it.

אֲנִי אֲחַכֶּה לָה.

ă-NEE ă-khă-KĔ lă.

663. Do you (PL.) have aspirin?

הַאִם יֵשׁ לָכֶם אַסְפִּירִין?

hă-EEM yĕsh lă-KHĔM ăs-pee-REEN?

LAUNDRY AND DRY CLEANING

664. Where is the [laundry]?

אֵיפֹה [הַמַּכְבֵּסָה]?

ay-FÓ [hă-măkh-bĕ-SÁ]?

665. —— a dry cleaner.

מַכְבֵּסָה לְנִקּוּי יָבֵשׁ.

măkh-bĕ-SÁ lᴗnee-KOOEY yă-VÉSH.

666. I want these shirts mended.

אֲבַקֵּשׁ לְתַקֵּן אֶת הַחֻלְצוֹת הָאֵלֶּה.*

ă-vă-KÉSH lᴗtă-KÉN ĕt hă-khool-TSÓT hă-É-lĕ.

667. I want these shirts washed [with starch].

אֲבַקֵּשׁ לְכַבֵּס אֶת הַחֻלְצוֹת הָאֵלֶּה [בַּעֲמִילָן].*

ă-vă-KÉSH lᴗkhă-BÉS ĕt hă-khool-TSÓT hă-É-lĕ [bă-ă-mee-LÁN].

668. —— without starch.

בְּלִי עֲמִילָן.

bᴗlee ă-mee-LÁN.

669. I want [this suit] cleaned and pressed.

אֲבַקֵּשׁ לְנַקּוֹת וּלְגַהֵץ [אֶת הַחֲלִיפָה הַזֹּאת].

ă-vă-KÉSH lᴗnă-KÓT oo-lᴗgă-HÉTS [ĕt hă-khă-lee-FÁ hă-ZÓT].

670. [The belt] is missing.

[הַחֲגוֹרָה] אֵינֶנָּה.

[hă-khă-gö-RÁ] ay-NÉ-nă.

671. Can you [sew on this button]?

הַאִם (תּוּכַל) (תּוּכְלִי) [לִתְפֹּר אֶת הַכַּפְתּוֹר הַזֶּה]?

hă-EEM (too-KHÁL ᴛᴏ ᴍ.) (too-KHᴗLEE ᴛᴏ ꜰ.) [leet-PÓR ĕt hă-kăf-TÓR hă-ZÉ]?

672. —— replace the zipper.

לְהַחֲלִיף אֶת הָרוֹכְסָן.

lᴗhă-khă-LEEF ĕt hă-rökh-SÁN.

BARBER SHOP AND BEAUTY SALON

673. Where is there [a barber shop] around here?

אֵיפֹה יֵשׁ כָּאן [מִסְפָּרָה]?

ay-FÓ yĕsh kăn [măs-pĕ-RÁ]?

*See footnote, page 42.

674. ———— a beauty salon.
מָכוֹן לְיֹפִי.
mă-KHŌN LYŌ-fee.

675. A haircut, please.
תִּסְפֹּרֶת, בְּבַקָּשָׁה.
tees-PŌ-rĕt, bvă-kă-SHĂ.

676. Please do not cut my hair [too short].
בְּבַקָּשָׁה לֹא לְסַפֵּר אֶת הַשְּׂעָרוֹת [קָצָר מְדַי].
bvă-kă-SHĂ lŏ lsă-PĒR ĕt hă-să-RŌT [kă-TSĂR mee-DĪ].

677. A shave.
גִּלּוּחַ.
gee-loo-ĂKH.

678. A shampoo.
חֲפִיפַת רֹאשׁ.
khă-fee-FĂT rösh.

679. A hair set.
תִּסְרֹקֶת.
tees-RŎ-kĕt.

680. A permanent.
סִלְסוּל תְּמִידִי.
seel-SOOL tmee-DEE.

681. A manicure.
מָנִיקְיוּר.
mă-neek-YOOR.

HEALTH AND ILLNESS: DOCTOR

682. I wish to call a doctor.
אֲנִי (רוֹצֶה) (רוֹצָה) לִקְרֹא [לְרוֹפֵא].
ă-NEE (rŏ-TSĚ m.) (ro-TSA f.) leek-RŌ [lrŏ-FĚ].

683. ———— an American doctor.
לְרוֹפֵא אָמֶרִיקָנִי.
lrŏ-FĚ ă-mĕ-ree-kă-NEE.

684. Is the doctor in?
הַאִם הָרוֹפֵא יֶשְׁנוֹ
hă-EEM hă-rŏ-FĚ yĕsh-NŎ?

685. I have [a headache].
יֵשׁ לִי [כְּאֵב רֹאשׁ].
yĕsh lee [kĕv rösh].

686. ———— an allergy.
אַלֶּרְגְּיָה.
ă-LĔRG-yă.

687. I have a cold.
אֲנִי (מְצֻנָּן) (מְצֻנֶּנֶת).
ă-NEE (mtsoo-NĂN m.) (mtsoo-NĚ-nĕt f.).

688. I have a cough.
אֲנִי (מִשְׁתַּעֵל) (מִשְׁתַּעֶלֶת).
ă-NEE (meesh-tă-ĚL m.) (meesh-tă-Ě-lĕt f.).

689. I have [constipation].
יֵשׁ לִי [עֲצִירוּת].
yĕsh lee [a-tsee-ROOT].

690. ———— diarrhea.
שִׁלְשׁוּל.
sheel-SHOOL.

691. ———— indigestion.
קֵבָה מְקֻלְקֶלֶת.
kĕ-VĂ mkool-KĚ-lĕt.

692. ———— pains in the stomach.
כְּאֵב בֶּטֶן.
kĕv BĚ-tĕn.

693. —— a pain in my chest.

כְּאֵב בֶּחָזֶה.

k‿ĕv bĕ‿khă-ZĔ.

694. —— a fever.

חֹם.

khŏm.

695. —— a sore throat.

כְּאֵב גָּרוֹן.

k‿ĕv gă-RŎN.

696. —— nausea.

בְּחִילָה.

b‿khee-LĂ.

697. I have something in my eye.

יֵשׁ לִי מַשֶּׁהוּ בָּעַיִן.

yĕsh lee MĂ-shĕ-hoo bă-Ă-yeen.

698. I did not sleep well.

לֹא יָשַׁנְתִּי הֵיטֵב.

lŏ yă-SHĂN-tee hay-TĔV.

699. How do you feel?

אֵיךְ (אַתָּה מַרְגִּישׁ) (אַתְּ מַרְגִּשָׁה)?

aykh (ă-TĂ măr-GEESH TO M.) (ăt măr-gee-SHĂ TO F.)?

700. I do not feel well.

אֵינֶנִּי (מַרְגִּישׁ) (מַרְגִּשָׁה) טוֹב.

ay-NĔ-nee (măr-GEESH M.) (măr-gee-SHĂ F.) tŏv.

701. I feel [well].

אֲנִי (מַרְגִּישׁ) (מַרְגִּשָׁה) [טוֹב].

ă-NEE (măr-GEESH M.) (măr-gee-SHĂ F.) [tŏv].

702. —— better.

יוֹתֵר טוֹב.

yŏ-TĔR tŏv.

703. —— worse.

יוֹתֵר רַע.

yŏ-TĔR ră.

704. Must I stay in bed?

הַאִם אֲנִי (מֻכְרָח) (מֻכְרָחָה) לִשְׁכַּב בַּמִּטָּה?

hă-EEM ă-NEE (mookh-RĂKH M.) (mookh-ră-KHĂ F.) leesh-KĂV bă-mee-TĂ?

705. When will I be able to travel again?

מָתַי אוּכַל לְהַמְשִׁיךְ בַּנְּסִיעָה?

mă-TĪ oo-KHĂL l‿hăm-SHEEKH bă-n‿see-Ă?

DENTIST

706. Do you know a good dentist?

הַאִם (אַתָּה מַכִּיר) (אַתְּ מַכִּירָה) רוֹפֵא שִׁנַּיִם טוֹב?

hă-EEM (ă-TĂ mă-KEER TO M.) (ăt mă-kee-RĂ TO F.) rŏ-FĔ shee-NĂ-yeem tŏv?

707. This tooth hurts.

הַשֵּׁן הַזֹּאת כּוֹאֶבֶת לִי.

hă-SHEN hă-ZŌT kŏ-Ē-vĕt lee.

708. Is it possible to treat it temporarily?

הַאִם אֶפְשָׁר לְטַפֵּל בָּה בְּאֹפֶן זְמַנִּי

hă-EEM ĕf-SHĂR l⌣tă-PĒL bă B⌣Ŏ-fĕn z⌣mă-NEE?

709. I seem to have lost a filling.

נָפְלָה לִי כַּנִּרְאֶה סְתִימָה.

nă-F⌣LĂ lee kă-neer-Ē s⌣tee-MĂ.

710. I don't want you to extract my tooth.

אֵינֶנִּי (רוֹצֶה) (רוֹצָה) שֶׁתַּעֲקֹר לִי אֶת הַשֵּׁן.

ay-NĒ-nee (rŏ-TSĒ m.) (rŏ-TSĂ f.) shĕ-tă-ă-KŎR lee ĕt hă-SHĒN.

SENDING A CABLEGRAM

711. אֲנִי רוֹצֶה לִשְׁלֹחַ מִבְרָק לְנִיוּ־יוֹרְק. מַה הַמְּחִיר ?

ă-NEE rŏ-TSĒ leesh-LŌ-ăkh meev-RĂK lee "New York." mă hă-M⌣KHEER?

I'd like to send a cablegram to New York City. What is the rate?

712. הַמְּחִיר שֶׁל מִבְרָק רָגִיל הוּא שְׁלוֹשִׁים וְחָמֵשׁ אֲגוֹרוֹת הַמִּלָּה.

hă-M⌣KHEER shĕl meev-RĂK ră-GEEL hoo sh⌣lŏ-SHEEM v⌣khă-MĒSH ă-gŏ-RŌT l⌣mee-LĂ.

The price of a regular cablegram is 35 agorot per word.

713. הַאִם קַיָּם אֶצְלְכֶם הַתַּשְׁלוּם הַמִּינִימָלִי בְּעַד עֶשֶׂר מִלִּים ?

hă-EEM kă-YĂM ĕts-L⌣KHĔM hă-tăsh-LOOM hă-mee-nee-mă-LEE b⌣ăd Ē-sĕr mee-LEEM?

Is there the usual ten-word minimum?

714. לֹא, אֵין אֶצְלֵנוּ תַּשְׁלוּם מִינִימָלִי. אַתָּה מְשַׁלֵּם בְּעַד כָּל מִלָּה, כּוֹלֵל הַשֵּׁם, הַכְּתֹבֶת וְהַחֲתִימָה.

lŏ, ayn ets-LĒ-noo tăsh-LOOM mee-nee-mă-LEE. ă-TĂ m⌣shă-LĒM b⌣ăd kŏl mee-LĂ, kŏ-LĒL hă-SHĒM, hă-K⌣TŌ-vĕt v⌣hă-khă-tee-MĂ.

No, there is no minimum rate. The charge is made for every word used, including the name, address and signature.

715. הַאִם אֶפְשָׁר לִשְׁלֹחַ מִבְרָק לַיְלָה?

hă-EEM ĕf-SHĂR leesh-LŎ-ăkh meev-RĂK LĪ-lă?

Is it possible to send a lettergram?

716. כֵּן, בַּחֲצִי הַמְּחִיר, אֲבָל הַתַּשְׁלוּם הַמִּינִימָלִי הוּא בְּעַד עֶשְׂרִים וּשְׁתַּיִם מִלָּה.

kĕn, bă-khă-TSEE hă-MᴗKHEER, ă-VĂL hă-tăsh-LOOM hă-mee-nee-mă-LEE hoo bᴗăd ĕs-REEM oo-SHᴗTĂ-yeem mee-LĂ.

Yes, at half rate, but the minimum charge is for 22 words.

717. מָתַי יַגִּיעַ מִבְרָק הַלַּיְלָה?

mă-TĪ yă-GEE-ă meev-RĂK hă-LĪ-la?

When will the lettergram arrive?

718. מָחָר אַחַר הַצָּהֳרַיִם.

mă-KHĂR ă-KHĂR hă-tsŏ-hŏ-RĂ-yeem.

Tomorrow afternoon.

719. מָתַי יַגִּיעַ הַמִּבְרָק הָרָגִיל?

mă-TĪ yă-GEE-ă hă-meev-RĂK hă-ră-GEEL?

When would the cablegram arrive?

720. תּוֹךְ חָמֵשׁ שָׁעוֹת.

tŏkh khă-MĔSH shă-ŎT.

Within five hours.

721. אֶשְׁלַח אִם כֵּן מִבְרָק רָגִיל.   הַאִם אוּכַל לְקַבֵּל כַּמָּה טְפָסִים?

ĕsh-LĂKH eem kĕn meev-RĂK ră-GEEL. hă-EEM oo-KHĂL ᴗkă-BĔL kă-MĂ ᴗfă-SEEM?

I'll send a regular cablegram.   May I have some forms?

722. הִנֵּה הֵם. כְּתֹב בְּבַקָּשָׁה אֶת הַשֵּׁם הַמָּלֵא וְהַכְּתֹבֶת בְּאוֹתִיּוֹת דְּפוּס. כַּאֲשֶׁר תָּבִיא אוֹתָם בַּחֲזָרָה, אֶשְׂמַח לְטַפֵּל בָּהֶם.

hee-NĔ hĕm. Kᴗ TŎV bᴗvă-kă-SHĂ ĕt hă-SHĔM hă-mă-LĔ vᴗhă-Kᴗ TŎ-vĕt bᴗŏ-tee-YŎT dᴗfoos. kă-ă-SHĔR tă-VEE ŏ-TĂM bă-khă-ză-RĂ, ĕs-MĂKH ᴗtă-PĔL bă-HĔM.

Here they are.   Please print your full name and address. When you bring these back, I'll be glad to take care of them.

723. תּוֹדָה רַבָּה.

tŏ-DĂ ră-BĂ.

Thanks very much.

52

TIME

724. What time is it?

מַה הַשָּׁעָה?

mă hă-shă-Ă?

725. It is very early.

הַשָּׁעָה מֻקְדֶּמֶת מְאֹד.

hă-shă-Ă mook-DĔ-mĕt m⌣ŏd.

726. It is quite late.

הַשָּׁעָה מְאֻחֶרֶת לְמַדַּי.

hă-shă-Ă m⌣oo-KHĔ-rĕt L⌣mă-DĬ.

727. It is almost two o'clock A.M.

הַשָּׁעָה כִּמְעַט שְׁתַּיִם בַּלַּיְלָה.

hă-shă-Ă keem-ĂT SH⌣TĂ-yeem bă-LĬ-lă.

728. It is half-past three P.M.

הַשָּׁעָה שָׁלוֹשׁ וָחֵצִי אַחַר הַצָּהֳרַיִם.

hă-shă-Ă shă-LŌSH vă-KHĔ-tsee ă-KHĂR hă-tsŏ-hŏ-RĂ-yeem.

729. It is a quarter past four.

הַשָּׁעָה אַרְבַּע וָרֶבַע.

hă-shă-Ă ăr-BĂ vă-RĔ-vă.

730. It is a quarter to five.

הַשָּׁעָה רֶבַע לְחָמֵשׁ.

hă-shă-Ă RĔ-vă L⌣khă-MĔSH.

731. At ten minutes to six.

בַּעֲשָׂרָה לְשֵׁשׁ.

bă-ă-să-RĂ L⌣shĕsh.

732. At twenty minutes past seven.

בְּשֶׁבַע וְעֶשְׂרִים.

B⌣SHĔ-vă v⌣ĕs-REEM.

733. In the morning.

בַּבֹּקֶר.

bă-BŎ-kĕr.

734. During the afternoon.

אַחַר הַצָּהֳרַיִם.

ă-KHĂR hă-tsŏ-hŏ-RĂ-yeem.

735. In the evening.

בָּעֶרֶב.

bă-Ĕ-rĕv.

736. Day.

יוֹם.

yŏm.

737. Every night.

כָּל לַיְלָה.

kŏl LĬ-lă.

738. Last night.

אֶמֶשׁ.

Ĕ-mĕsh.

739. Last month.

בַּחֹדֶשׁ שֶׁעָבַר.

bă-KHŎ-dĕsh shĕ-ă-VĂR.

740. Last year.

בַּשָּׁנָה שֶׁעָבְרָה.

bă-shă-NĂ shĕ-ă-V⌣RĂ.

741. Yesterday.

אֶתְמוֹל.

ĕt-MŌL.

742. Today.

הַיּוֹם.

hă-YŌM.

743. Tonight.

הַלַּיְלָה.

hă-LĬ-lă.

744. Tomorrow.
מָחָר.
mă-KHĂR.

745. Next week.
בַּשָּׁבוּעַ הַבָּא.
bă-shă-VOO-ă hă-BĂ.

DAYS OF THE WEEK

746. Sunday.
יוֹם רִאשׁוֹן.
yŏm ree-SHŌN.

747. Monday.
יוֹם שֵׁנִי.
yŏm shĕ-NEE.

748. Tuesday.
יוֹם שְׁלִישִׁי.
yŏm shlee-SHEE.

749. Wednesday.
יוֹם רְבִיעִי.
yŏm rvee-EE.

750. Thursday.
יוֹם חֲמִישִׁי.
yŏm khă-mee-SHEE.

751. Friday.
יוֹם שִׁשִּׁי.
yŏm shee-SHEE.

752. Saturday.
שַׁבָּת.
shă-BĂT.

MONTHS

753. January.
יָנוּאָר.
YĂ-noo-ăr.

754. February.
פֶּבְּרוּאָר.
FĔB-roo-ăr.

755. March.
מַרְס.
mărs.

756. April.
אַפְּרִיל.
ăp-REEL.

757. May.
מַאי.
mĭ.

758. June.
יוּנִי.
YOO-nee.

759. July.
יוּלִי.
YOO-lee.

760. August.
אוֹגוּסְט.
ŏ-GOOST.

761. September.
סֶפְּטֶמְבֶּר.
sĕp-TĔM-bĕr.

762. October.
אוֹקְטוֹבֶּר.
ŏk-TŌ-bĕr.

763. November.
נוֹבֶמְבֶּר.
nŏ-VĔM-bĕr.

764. December.
דֶצֶמְבֶּר.
dĕ-TSĔM-bĕr.

SEASONS AND WEATHER

765. Spring.
אָבִיב.
ă-VEEV.

766. Summer.
קַיִץ.
KĂ-yeets.

767. Autumn.
סְתָו.
s-tăv.

768. Winter.
חֹרֶף.
KHŌ-rĕf.

769. It is warm.
חַם.
khăm.

770. It is cold.
קַר.
kăr.

771. The weather is [good].

מֶזֶג־הָאֲוִיר [נָאֶה].

MĔ-zĕg hă-ă-VEER [nă-Ĕ].

772. —— bad.

נָרוּעַ.

gă-ROO-ă.

773. The sun is shining.

הַשֶּׁמֶשׁ זוֹרַחַת.

hă-SHĔ-mĕsh ză-RĂ-khăt.

774. A wind is blowing.

נוֹשֶׁבֶת רוּחַ.

nă-SHĔ-vĕt ROO-ăkh.

775. It is still raining.

עֲדַיִן יוֹרֵד גֶּשֶׁם.

ă-DĂ-yeen yă-RĔD GĔ-shĕm.

776. It is snowing.

יוֹרֵד שֶׁלֶג.

yă-RĔD SHĔ-lĕg.

777. What is the weather forecast [for tomorrow]?

מַה תַּחֲזִית מֶזֶג־הָאֲוִיר [לְמָחָר]?

MĂ tă-khă-ZEET MĔ-zĕg hă-ă-VEER [ᴗmă-KHĂR]?

NUMBERS*

778. One.

(אַחַת) (אֶחָד).

(ă-KHĂT F.) (ĕ-KHĂD M.).

Two.

(שְׁתַּיִם) (שְׁנַיִם).

(SHᴗTĂ-yeem F.) (SHᴗNA-yeem M.)

Three.

(שָׁלוֹשׁ) (שְׁלוֹשָׁה).

(shă-LŌSH F.), (shᴗlŏ-SHĂ M.).

Four.

(אַרְבַּע) (אַרְבָּעָה).

(ăr-BĂ F.), (ăr-bă-Ă M.).

Five.

(חָמֵשׁ) (חֲמִשָּׁה).

(khă-MĔSH F.), (khă-mee-SHĂ M.).

Six.

(שֵׁשׁ) (שִׁשָּׁה).

(shĕsh F.), (shee-SHĂ M.).

Seven.

(שֶׁבַע) (שִׁבְעָה).

(SHĔ-vă F.), (sheev-Ă M.).

Eight.

(שְׁמוֹנֶה) (שְׁמוֹנָה).

(shᴗmŏ-NĔ F.), (shᴗmŏ-NĂ M.).

Nine.

(תֵּשַׁע) (תִּשְׁעָה).

(TĔ-shă F.), (teesh-Ă M.).

Ten.

(עֶשֶׂר) (עֲשָׂרָה).

(Ĕ-ser F.), (ă-să-RĂ M.).

Eleven.

(אַחַת עֶשְׂרֵה) (אַחַד עָשָׂר).

(ă-KHĂT ĕs-RĔ F.), (ă-KHĂD ă-SĂR M.).

Twelve.

(שְׁתֵּים עֶשְׂרֵה) (שְׁנֵים עָשָׂר).

(shᴗtaym ĕs-RĔ F.), (shᴗnaym ă-SĂR M.).

---

*The masculine form (m.) is the form used with masculine nouns; the feminine form (f.) is used with feminine nouns. The use of masculine or feminine gender does not refer to the sex of the speaker. When only one form appears, it can be used with either masculine or feminine nouns. Note that the feminine form which appears first and is spoken is always used for counting.

Thirteen.
(שְׁלוֹשׁ עֶשְׂרֵה) (שְׁלוֹשָׁה עָשָׂר).
(sh‿lósh ĕs-RĔ F.), (sh‿lo-SHĂ ă-SĂR M.).

Fourteen.
(אַרְבַּע עֶשְׂרֵה) (אַרְבָּעָה עָשָׂר).
(ăr-BĂ ĕs-RĔ F.), (ăr-bă-Ă ă-SĂR M.).

Fifteen.
(חֲמֵשׁ עֶשְׂרֵה) (חֲמִשָּׁה עָשָׂר).
(khă-MĔSH ĕs-RĔ F.), (khă-mee-SHĂ ă-SĂR M.).

Sixteen.
(שֵׁשׁ עֶשְׂרֵה) (שִׁשָּׁה עָשָׂר).
(shĕsh ĕs-RĔ F.), (shee-SHĂ ă-SĂR M.).

Seventeen.
(שְׁבַע עֶשְׂרֵה) (שִׁבְעָה עָשָׂר).
(sh‿vă ĕs-RĔ F.), (sheev-Ă ă-SĂR M.).

Eighteen.
(שְׁמוֹנֶה עֶשְׂרֵה) (שְׁמוֹנָה עָשָׂר).
(sh‿mŏ-NĔ ĕs-RĔ F.), (sh‿mŏ-NĂ ă-SĂR M.).

Nineteen.
(תְּשַׁע עֶשְׂרֵה) (תִּשְׁעָה עָשָׂר).
(t‿shă ĕs-RĔ F.), (teesh-Ă ă-SĂR M.).

Twenty.
עֶשְׂרִים.
ĕs-REEM.

Twenty-one.
(עֶשְׂרִים וְאַחַת) (עֶשְׂרִים וְאֶחָד).
(ĕs-REEM v‿ă-KHĂT F.), ĕs-REEM v‿ĕ-KHĂD M.).

Twenty-two.
(עֶשְׂרִים וּשְׁתַּיִם) (עֶשְׂרִים וּשְׁנַיִם).
(ĕs-REEM oo-SH‿TĂ-yeem F.), (ĕs-REEM oo-SH‿NĂ-yeem M.).

Thirty.
שְׁלוֹשִׁים.
sh‿lŏ-SHEEM.

Forty.
אַרְבָּעִים.
ăr-bă-EEM.

Fifty.
חֲמִשִּׁים.
khă-mee-SHEEM.

Sixty.
שִׁשִּׁים.
shee-SHEEM.

Seventy.
שִׁבְעִים.
sheev-EEM.

Eighty.
שְׁמוֹנִים.
sh‿mŏ-NEEM.

Ninety.
תִּשְׁעִים.
teesh-EEM.

One hundred.
מֵאָה.
mĕ-Ă.

One hundred one.
מֵאָה וְאַחַת.
mĕ-Ă v‿ă-KHĂT.

Two hundred.
מָאתַיִם.
mă-TĂ-yeem.

Three hundred.
שְׁלוֹשׁ מֵאוֹת.
sh‿lŏsh mĕ-ŎT.

Four hundred.
אַרְבַּע מֵאוֹת.
ăr-BĂ mĕ-ŎT.

One thousand.
אֶלֶף.
É-lĕf.

Two thousand.
אַלְפַּיִם.
ăl-PĂ-yeem.

Three thousand.
שְׁלוֹשֶׁת אֲלָפִים.
SH⌣LŎ-shĕt ă-lă-FEEM.

Four thousand.
אַרְבַּעַת אֲלָפִים.
ăr-bă-ĂT ă-lă-FEEM.

One million.
מִלְיוֹן.
meel-YŎN.

Two million.
שְׁנֵי מִלְיוֹן.
sh⌣nay meel-YŎN.

INDEX

The sentences, words and phrases in this book are numbered consecutively from 1 to 778. All entries in this book refer to these numbers. In addition, each major section heading (CAPITALIZED) is indexed according to page number (**boldface**). Parts of speech are indicated by the following italic abbreviations: *adj.* for adjective, *adv.* for adverb, *n.* for noun, *prep.* for preposition and *v.* for verb. Parentheses are used for explanations.

Because of the large volume of material indexed, cross-indexing has generally been avoided. Phrases or groups of words will usually be found under only one of their components, e.g., "bathing suit" appears only under "bathing," even though there is a separate entry for "suit" alone. If you do not find a phrase under one word, try another.

dressing (salad) 454
drink *n.* 320; *v.* 317
drive 223
driver 218
driver's license 227
DRUGSTORE **p. 46**
drugstore 625
dry cleaner 665
duck 392
during 734
duty (customs) 135

Early 725
earrings 596
east 155
eat 344
egg 381, 384
eight 778
eighteen 778
eighty 778
elevator 274
eleven 778
engine 246
English (language) 59
English-speaking 462
enjoy oneself 25
entrance 487
envelope 644
especially 446
evening *adj.* 500; *n.* 3;
   good — 3; in the —
   735
every 737
everything 131
excellent 359
excess 205
exchange rate 519
excuse me 81
exit *n.* 488
export, for 563
extract *v.* 710
eyeglasses 117

Family 23
far, how 161
farm: collective — 480;
   cooperative — 481
fat (rich food) 347
father, my 12
February 754
feel 527, 700; how do
   you — 699
fever 694
few, a 141
fifteen 778
fifty 778
fill 239; — out 537

filling (dental) 709
film 655, 656
find 112
finish 138
fish *n.* 389
fishing, go 512
five 778
flight 203
FOOD **p. 26**
food 359
foreign 515
forget 114
fork 339
form 537
forty 778
forward *v.* 299
four 778
fourteen 778
fragile 534
free (= available) 220
Friday 751
fried 348, 383
friend 46, 111
from 443
fruit 431; — cup (= sal-
   ad) 452; — juice 375
FRUITS **p. 28**
furnished 253

Galilee, Sea of 147
gallon 237
garage 229
garlic 371
gas station 228
GENERAL
   EXPRESSIONS **p. 5**
get 353; — off 218
gift 134
girl 91
give 237
glass 319, 434
gloves 569
go 163, 189
good 231, 771
goodbye (= peace) 5
gram 527
grape 423
grapefruit 422
gray 612
green 613
grocery 626
guide 470
guidebook 639

Habima theater 483
Haifa 148
hair 676; — set 679

haircut 675
half 422; — past 728
handbag 570
handle *v.* 142
happen 125
hard-boiled 382
hardware store 628
hat 571
have 256, 257
he 47
headache 685
headwaiter 333
health: — certificate 126;
   to your — (= to life)
   326
HEALTH AND
   ILLNESS: DOCTOR
   p. 48
hear 505
Hebrew (language) 61
hello (= peace) 1; (tele-
   phone) 307
help *n.* 180; *v.* 109
here 48, 213; come —
   102; — is 123
herring 387; marinated
   — 452
hill 178
horseback riding, go 513
hotel 250, 296
HOTEL AND APART-
   MENT **p. 17**
hour 141; per — 221
how 99; — are you 20;
   — far 161; — long
   (time) 146; — many
   204; — much 136
hundred: one — 778; two
   — 778
hungry, I am 52
hurry, I am in a 51
hurt 707
husband 10

I 40
ice 361; — cream 441
identification card 125
if 335
immediately 661
important, most 476
include 298
including 714
indigestion 691
inexpensive 251
inside 534
instead of 353
instrument, musical 597

open *v.* 131; (establish-
ment) 485
opera, to the 494
opposite *adj.* 167; *prep.*
176
orange (color) 614; (fruit)
425; → juice 376
order *n.* 448; *v.* 352, 553
overheat 246
owe 529

Pack *n.* 651
package 141
pain 692
painting, in 474
pair 579
paper: toilet — 291; writing — 645
parcel post 530
park (*n.* = public garden)
176; *v.* 248
pass 363
passport 124
pastry 457
pay *v.* 136
pea 408
peace 35
peach 427
pear 426
pen, fountain 646
pencil 647
pepper (seasoning) 368;
(vegetable) 409
performance 500
perfume 598
perhaps 79
permanent *n.* 680
personal 130
PERSONAL MATTERS
p. 2
pharmacist 660
pharmacy 659
picture 599
pie 439
piece 428
pillow 285
pillowcase 286
pink 615
place 255, 467
plane *adj.* 197
plate 341
play *n.* 460; (*v.,* theater)
498
please 80
pleased 57
P.M. (= in the afternoon)
728

policeman 120
police station 119
poor (quality) 308
port (harbor) 148
porter 276
possible 505; if — 335
postage (= stamps) 524
postcard 648
POST OFFICE
CONVERSATION
p. 37
potash works 484
potato 410–412
pottery 600
pound (currency) 520
prefer 255
prescription 661
press *v.* 669
price 545
priest 463
properly 245
Protestant 467
purple 616
purse 113
purser 192

Quarter: — past 279, 729;
— to 730
quiet 255
quite 726

Rabbi 462
radiator 239
railroad station 206
raining, it is 775
raincoat 574
rare (meat) 350
raspberry 429
rate 714
read 60
ready 557
receipt 538
recommend 327
record (phonograph) 601
red 617
regards (= give regards)
26
registration 537
rent 226
repair 244
repeat 70
replace 672
reservation 197, 200, 256
reserved 186
residential section, to the
150
restaurant 327

RESTAURANT, AT THE
p. 23
RESTAURANT
CONVERSATION
p. 30
rice 413
right (= correct) 163; to
the — 157
road 179
roast *adj.* 391
roll (bread) 364
room 257, 271; double
— 259; — number
295; — service (= ser-
vice) 275; single —
258; waiting — 187

Sabbath 35
safe deposit box 262
salad 353
salesgirl 559
salesman 560
salt 367
sardine 388
Saturday 752
say, how do you 75
school 177
sculpture, in 475
sea 147
SEASONS AND
WEATHER **p. 53**
seat 186; balcony — 503;
box — 504; orchestra
— 502
see 271; — you later 6
send 276
SENDING A CABLE-
GRAM **p. 50**
September 761
serve 331
service 275; — charge
355
seven 778
seventeen 778
seventy 778
several 269
sew 671
shade (color) 607
shampoo 678
sharp 458
shave 677
sheet 288
sherry 319
shine 773
ship 558
shirt 585, 666
shoe 576; — store 632

shoelace 577
SHOPPING **p. 39**
short 148, 676
shorts 586; (underwear) 588
show *v.* 149, 236
shower 266
side 166
SIGHTSEEING **p. 33**
sign *v.* 539
signature 714
silk 605
silver 594
silverware 602
sir 461
sister, my 16
sit down 24
six 778
sixteen 778
sixty 778
skirt 578
sleep 698
slipper 579
slowly, more 62
small 522
smaller 550
smoke *v.* 213
snowing, it is 776
soap 289
soccer game, to the 510
SOCIAL CONVERSA-TION **p. 1**
socks 580
soda water 318
soft-boiled 381
something 317
son, my 14
soon (= at once) 276; as — as possible 297
sorry, I am 56
soup: chicken — 385; vegetable — 386
SOUPS AND ENTRÉES **p. 27**
south, to the 154
souvenir 603
speak 58, 292
spicy 345
spinach 414
spoon, large 343
SPORTS **p. 35**
spring (season) 765
stall *v.* 247
starch 668
start 500
stationer 636
stay 254

steak 396
steward 191
still 775
stocking 581
stomach 692
stop *v.* 188, 216
store 621; department — 624
STORES **p. 43**
strawberry 430
street 159
stronger 551
student: college — 42; high school — 43
subway 216
sugar 366
suit 582, 669
suite 261
summer 766
sun 773
Sunday 746
supper 331
sweater 583
sweet 346
swimming, go 514
swimming pool 511
synagogue 465, 477

Table 335
tailor 633
tasty 447
tax 298
TAXI **p. 15**
taxi 219
tea 435
teacher 44
teaspoon 342
Technion 216
Tel Aviv, to 139
telephone *v.* 132
TELEPHONE CON-VERSATION **p. 21**
tell 110, 218
temporarily 708
ten 778
thanks 180; — very much 82
that 73
theater 483
then 280
there 162; from — 505
these 357
thing 135; same — 553
think so 69
thirsty, I am 53
thirteen 778
thirty 778

this 74, 234
thousand 778
three 778
throat, sore 695
Thursday 750
Tiberias 146
ticket: one-way — 183; round-trip — 182; — window 181
TICKETS **p. 12**
TIME **p. 52**
time: at what — 202; on — 203; what — is it 724
tire *n.* 243; flat — 244
tired, I am 55
toast 379
tobacco: pipe — 653; — store 622
today 742
token 217
tomato 415; — juice 377
tomorrow 744
tonight 743
too (overly) 345
tooth 707
total *adj.* 537
tourist *adj.* 639; — office 145
towel 290
town 234
toy 604
track 208
traffic light 170
TRAIN **p. 14**
train 207; express — 185; local — 184
travel 50; — agent's office 144
TRAVEL DIRECTIONS **p. 10**
treat *v.* 708
trousers 587
trunk 132
try on 552
Tuesday 748
turn 153
twelve 778
twenty 778
twenty-one 778
twenty-two 778
two 778

Umbrella 605
uncle, to your 26
undershirt 589
understand 63, 659